dedication

THIS VOLUME IS ALSO FOR MY PAT.
HER LOVE INSPIRED THESE PLAYS.
HER WARMTH INFORMS THEM STILL.

Testosterone and Other One-Act Plays
by Albert Meglin

Testosterone

Emily, On Her Glider

Miss Monroe Explains

The Band Takes A Short Break

Two Sisters Sitting On A Bench,
Resting From All The Excitement

Luncheon With Mr. Mozart

The Visiting Room

On A West Side Roof, 1 in the Afternoon

stage plays

STAGEPLAYS THEATRE COMPANY
1674 Broadway, Suite 401
New York, New York 10019
Telephone: (212) 354-7565
Telefax: (212) 354-7585
www.stageplaystheatre.com

Testosterone and Other One-Act Plays by Albert Meglin
ISBN 0-9754851-5-6

Published by Stageplays Theatre Company

Design, Layout & Photograph: Doug Barron

First Edition, July 2009

Printed in the United States of America.

BY WAY OF FURTHER INTRODUCTION

I can't tell you precisely when I began to think of the one-act play as a nearly impossible, if quite wonderful, literary form. It is my fortune and my misfortune both to love it, for it is one tough nut to crack!

The one-act play is a compact, concise thing indeed, and the challenges it offers a writer are legion. First of all, it takes place in real time. There is no way of dispelling a mood or devising a plot turn with easy instructions like "Three weeks later," no way of shifting to a more exotic locale or a more dramatic new climate with handy stage directions like "Jeremy's other villa on a sultry August night." No, there is no tempering, no unraveling of dilemma, except in the here and now. When the curtain goes up on a one-act play, the characters are before you, and there they remain, to connect and intertwine. Whatever the pickle you've given them, that's the pickle they'll deal with. Economically. Very economically.

Altogether, no small task, yes?

Over the years, I like to think I've learned a bit about writing all sorts of plays, full-length plays, comedies, dramas. But I still find one-act plays the most challenging and therefore the most rewarding to huddle over. I still enjoy getting my characters into a tight spot and out of it in as few pages as possible.

So there you have it then: a life-long obsession with one-act plays.

I hope you enjoy reading the plays in this volume, too.

A. M.

contents

TESTOSTERONE

a one-act play

Testosterone

setting:
A commuter train.
A bank of passenger seats, located in the corner nearest the door which connects to the next car. The door is tied open to allow air to circulate, given the air-conditioning malfunction.

time:
The present, a hot summer evening.

characters:
JOSH
the settled commuter, about 45

BRAD
the macho yuppie, about 35

DIRK
the youngest pup, about 25

LYDIA LOPATKIN
the big-haired, well-built NYU student in the cut-off tank top, about 20

AT RISE: JOSH *enters, with long ambassadorial umbrella and atta-ché case.* HE *wipes his forehead with a handkerchief.* HE *goes to the leftmost (window) seat and puts his gear under it.* HE *removes his jacket, and, folding it carefully, places it on the middle seat.*

HE *sits. Pulling a pad from his pocket,* HE *makes a note or two.*

Now BRAD *enters, with short compact umbrella and laptop.* HE, *too, is sweating mightily.* HE *goes to the rightmost (aisle) seat and puts his gear under it.* HE *sits.* HE *removes his shoes and, unnoticed by* JOSH, *puts them atop the folded jacket.*

The two men do not engage. Individually, JOSH *and* BRAD *pull out their cell phones.* THEY *are about to make calls when* LYDIA *enters through the far door. In a chopped-off tank top and shorts,* SHE *carries an upscale shopping bag.* SHE *also has a small portable fan.* SHE *runs her fan over her arms and neck.* JOSH *and* BRAD, *still not acknowledging each other, are entranced.*

BRAD: *(Still staring at* LYDIA*)* This car is a hotbox.

JOSH: *(Still staring at* LYDIA*)* The next one is air-conditioned.

BRAD: *(Still staring at* LYDIA*)* It's also jammed.

Beat

There's no *air* in here.

JOSH: *(Still staring at* LYDIA*)* The door is tied open.

BRAD: *(Still staring at* LYDIA*)* What good is *that*?

JOSH: *(Still staring at* LYDIA*)* There'll be a breeze when the train starts up again.

BRAD: *(Still staring at* LYDIA, *unaware of repeating himself)* This car is a hotbox.

JOSH: *(Still staring at* LYDIA, *unaware of repeating himself)* The next one is air-conditioned.

But LYDIA *finds this car too hot.* SHE *smiles at* JOSH *and* BRAD; *then* SHE *exits.* JOSH *and* BRAD *watch the departure disappointedly. Each breathes a deep sigh. Finally,* THEY *get down to business on their cell phones.*

Into his cell phone.

Hello, Vi?...Josh...Don't ask! The train is sitting outside some station, Woodbine, I think. We're running late. About–

HE *looks at his watch.*

– 45 minutes. You wouldn't believe the heat, but at least I'm sitting down...No, I've got some work to do. So how are the kids?

BRAD: *(Into his cell phone)* Hey, Marty! Brad here. How ya doin', guy?...What *I'm* doin' is sweltering on this nowhere train...Outside some station...Who knows?

To JOSH, *barely looking at him.*

What station?

JOSH: *(Barely looking at* BRAD*)* Woodbine, I think.

BRAD: *(Into his cell phone)* Woodbine, he thinks. Listen, your high-powered bash may have to do without big Brad for a while – this train is *not* budging!...I don't know, Marty. I don't know which one will be on my arm, because I have done a dumb thing: I have asked them *both*...Yeah, the Leggy One and Babycakes *both*!...Well, the Leggy One is a doll, sensible and all, but *Babycakes*! That girl has gotten *very* wild. You wouldn't believe – what? *(HE laughs)* Good training from big Brad, you got *that* right!

JOSH: *(Intrigued,* HE *reluctantly returns to his own call)* But why did you give her this number, Vi?...I *hate* to talk with her...Because she's a dragon lady. All she says is "I speak for Doctor, you know." I *hate* that...It *can't* be time for another payment! What is he, an orthodontist or a loan shark?...Vi, your daughter's teeth were straighter *before* he got his stubby hands on them!...I *will* tell her!...I'll tell *whoever*!

BRAD: *(First sign of engagement)* Whomever.

JOSH: What?

BRAD: Whomever. The word you want is "whomever".

JOSH: *(Giving* BRAD *an angry stare,* HE *returns to his call)* So how are the kids?

BRAD: *(Into his cell phone)* It's this way, Marty: I don't *like* to disappoint the Leggy One, but I could go for a repeat tonight with Babycakes!...What? Forty-five minutes, he thinks.

HE *looks at* JOSH'S *watch and taps his arm.*

Timex, right?

JOSH: What?

BRAD: *This* is a Rolex.

HE *shows* JOSH *his watch, then returns to his call.*

We're running 54 minutes, 33 seconds late. I'll see you when I see you, okay? Right now I'm snatching me a couple of Zs.

JOSH: *(Into his cell phone)* I'll see you when I see you, okay? Right now, I've got Mr. Wesley's return to look over.

JOSH *and* BRAD *put away their cell phones.* JOSH *readies his attaché case.*

BRAD: *(Eyes closed)* Big Brad needs his Zs, because he got no sleep last night.

JOSH: The Leggy One?

BRAD: Babycakes.

JOSH: Babycakes! Right! So, make it up tonight, big Brad.

BRAD: *(Yawning)* You sound like the sensible one.

JOSH: Babycakes?

BRAD: The Leggy One.

JOSH: The Leggy One! Right! I get them mixed up sometimes.

Now HE *spots the shoes atop his jacket.*

Hey!

BRAD: *(Opening his eyes)* What?

JOSH *points to the shoes.*

You mind?

JOSH: Hell, yes, I mind!

HE *picks up the shoes, about to drop them to the floor.*

BRAD: *(Taking* JOSH'S *arm)* Those are Brazilian lizard, friend!

JOSH: *(Pointing to his jacket)* Italian silk, friend!

BRAD: Italian silk is *out*, friend!

JOSH: Brazilian lizard is endangered, friend!

BRAD: It's *not* endangered. It's scarce.

JOSH: *(Dropping the shoes)* Now it's scarcer!

BRAD *scampers to the floor for his shoes.* JOSH *moves his jacket to make room for the shoes.* BRAD *places them. Then* HE *puts his head back to snooze.*

JOSH *looks through his attaché case impatiently.*

Damn!

HE *calls on his cell phone.*

Hello, Mona? I'm glad I caught you! I need to ask a favor, okay? E-mail the last 7 pages of the new limited partnership tax rules to me, would you? I thought I had them, but – what? Mr. Wesley is coming at 7 AM and–

Getting increasingly annoyed.

Mona! I don't tell a client when to come, he tells *me*! That's the way it works!

BRAD: *(Eyes closed again)* That is *not* the way it works.

JOSH: What?

BRAD: Clients don't tell *me* when to come, I tell *them*!

JOSH: Funny! I thought I was having a private conversation.

BRAD: Look – I'll show you.

HE *dials on his cell phone.*

Your first mistake is having a secretary named Mona! Secretaries should be named–

Into the cell phone.

Crystal, honey!

To JOSH

You wouldn't believe her cup size!

Into the cell phone.

Listen, Crystal, honey, the theatre tickets with Mr. and Mrs. Bernard tomorrow night? Cancel *mine*, okay? I won't be in any shape to give up my evening for them…What?…Tell them anything you want, only do this for big Brad, Crystal, honey!…Great!

HE *ends his call and turns to* JOSH.

And *that's* how it works!

JOSH: The mover-and-shaker in lizard shoes!

Into his cell phone.

No, not you, Mona. Did you find – ? Okay, good! E-mail them right away! Thanks, Mona.

HE *exits his phone and turns to* BRAD.

I will *always* give up my evening for a client. It's called a sense of – what is that word? Oh, yes, "responsibility." You've heard of it? Maybe not.

JOSH *writes notes on his pad.* BRAD *shrugs and prepares to close his eyes.*

Suddenly, however, LYDIA *reappears. This time* SHE *works her portable fan on her legs, one, then the other, slowly.*

Once again, JOSH *and* BRAD *are entranced.*

BRAD: Do you see that?

JOSH: I see it.

BRAD: That's awesome.

JOSH: That's weird.

More quietly.

No. Awesome. *Awesome* is what it is.

This time, LYDIA *waves at* JOSH *and* BRAD; *then,* SHE *leaves the car: it is too hot for her here.*

BRAD: Maybe I'll just go into that car and check that out.

JOSH: Better you should rest for the Leggy One.

BRAD: Or Babycakes.

JOSH: Whoever.

BRAD: *Whomever.* Trust me on this.

JOSH: *(Impatiently)* Why the hell isn't this train *moving*?

JOSH writes notes. BRAD *closes his eyes. There is a moment of silence. Then the sound of a cell phone interrupts. There is some awkwardness as* THEY *figure out whose cell phone is ringing. It turns out to be* JOSH'S.

Into his cell phone.

Hello?...Oh, yes, how are you? ...No, no trouble at all. You speak for Doctor, do I have that right?

BRAD: Would I believe Dragon Lady's cup size?

JOSH: *(Into the cell phone)* But it *can't* be time for another payment. What is Doctor, an orthodontist or a loan shark?...That was a joke, Miss.... Only a joke. I...

Now BRAD'S *cell phone rings.* BRAD *finds it and answers.*

BRAD: *(Into his cell phone)* Hello?...Janice! What a nice surprise!

To JOSH

The ex-wife.

JOSH: Would I believe her cup size?

BRAD: That was good. *Very* good!

Into the cell phone.

So what can I do you for?...It *can't* be the end of the month, Janice, old girl We just *had* the end of the month...I sent the check two weeks ago...All right, two days ago...It *can't* have bounced!... Okay, so it bounced!

JOSH: *(Toward* BRAD's *cell phone)* Those Brazilian lizard checks *will* do that, Janice, old girl!

Into his cell phone.

Has Doctor thought of buying rubber bands in job lots for my daughter's mouth?

A sickly laugh.

That was just another joke, Miss...It will be in the mail tomorrow... Okay, tonight!...I am *not* one of those, Miss –!

BRAD: *(Toward* JOSH's *cell phone)* He *is* one of those, Dragon Lady!!

JOSH *shoots* BRAD *an angry look.* JOSH *ends his call and puts his cell phone away.*

Into his cell phone.

What?...No, I have not forgotten my own son's birthday!...I *have* bought a present...Well, I haven't bought it exactly, I've been thinking about it...When *is* his birthday?...I *have* it written down at home, but I am *not* at home!...You know what, Janice, old girl? I think I'll stop accepting calls from the world's bitter people!

HE *exits his cell phone.*

JOSH: Janice, old girl, "one." Big Brad, "zero."

A hostile look at JOSH *from* BRAD. *Now, turning away from the other, each calls on his cell phone again.*

Into his cell phone.

Hello, Vi? She called!...What's *with* Doctor, anyway? Is he using gold bullion in those braces?

BRAD: *(Toward* JOSH's *cell phone)* That was a joke, Vi!

Into his cell phone.

Hello, Crystal, honey? One more thing. I want you to transfer some cash into my checking account, okay? ...Well, sure, I could do it if I had my laptop with me, but it is *not* with me, Crystal, honey!

JOSH: *(Toward* BRAD's *cell phone)* That laptop is in full view, Crystal, honey!

BRAD *shoots* JOSH *an ugly look.*

Into his cell phone.

Okay, then, listen, Vi: there isn't enough in the regular account. Write Doctor a check from MasterCard, okay? ...The *silver* MasterCard account. You know the one.

BRAD: *(Into his cell phone)* Two hundred at least, Crystal, honey. I have a present to buy. Transfer it from my *gold* MasterCard account. You know the one.

JOSH: *(Into his cell phone)* No, wait, Vi! Write the check from the *platinum* Visa account.

BRAD: *(Into his cell phone)* No, wait, Crystal, honey! Transfer it from my *platinum-plus* Visa account.

JOSH & BRAD: *(Simultaneously into their respective cell phones)* Better yet, from the American Express *titanium* account!

JOSH & BRAD *exchange hostile glances.*

BRAD: *(Into his cell phone)* Crystal, honey! What's taking so long?

JOSH: *(Into his cell phone)* What? *Whomever's* name is on the card.

BRAD: Whoever's.

JOSH: Aggh!

Into his cell phone.

I wasn't saying "Aggh" to you. I was saying "Aggh" to someone else! What? ...No, I haven't done anything about the car...Vi, what's the rush? He doesn't start college for two months. He can do without a car until...Okay...Okay! I *will!* Yes. *Now!*

HE *ends his call.*

BRAD: *(Into his cell phone)* Good girl! Mucho thanks, Crystal, honey!

HE *ends his call. Then* HE *turns to* JOSH.

Your kid needs to show off his wheels to friends *before* he goes to school. It's a macho thing. Too old to remember, pal?

JOSH: You're getting to be a pain in my keester, you know that, pal?

BRAD: Oh, yeah?

JOSH: Yeah!

BRAD: Oh, yeah?

JOSH: Yeah! If it weren't for this open door, I'd move!

BRAD: If it weren't for the breeze we'll get, *I'd* move!

JOSH: Oh, yeah?

BRAD: Yeah!

JOSH: Oh, yeah?

BRAD: Yeah!

Suddenly, LYDIA *reappears.* SHE *works her portable fan across her waist and under the tank top.* SHE *sighs in relief.*

JOSH *and* BRAD *are mesmerized. This time,* LYDIA *blows a kiss at* JOSH *and* BRAD *before* SHE *leaves the car.*

Did you see that?

JOSH: I saw it.

BRAD: That is someone big Brad could curl up with! Is that someone old Josh could curl up with?

JOSH: *(Quietly)* In my dreams, maybe.

BRAD: What?

JOSH: *(Aloud)* I said, in *your* dreams, maybe.

JOSH *and* BRAD *fall into individual reveries, anger and competitiveness subsiding for a moment.* THEY *sit back. Then, reality intruding,* THEY *dial on their cell phones simultaneously.*

BRAD: *(Into his cell phone)* Hello? Let me talk to Sal, please... Brad.

To JOSH

My brother's place – fifth-biggest sporting goods store in the Tri-State Area.

JOSH: Not fourth-biggest?

BRAD: Any day now, my man!

JOSH: *(Into his cell phone)* Hello? Irv, please...Josh.

To BRAD

My brother-in-law – past vice-president of the Automotive Dealers Association in the Four-State Area. Any car I want, 28% off sticker price.

BRAD: You jest, right? *Every* hungry salesman gives 28% off sticker price!

JOSH: You don't listen! I said *38%*!

BRAD: *(Into his cell phone)* Look! Tell him Brad needs a birthday present for the kid.

To JOSH

He has a birthday next week. Or last week. Or *this* week.

JOSH: He's not picky, I see.

BRAD: No! He's not!

JOSH: My kid needs to show off his wheels to friends before he goes to school.

BRAD: I just said that!

JOSH: I *thought* it first.

BRAD: My kid's growing up fast! He's five. Or maybe six. Or maybe even seven.

JOSH: My kid's off to community college and he's not 18 till November!

BRAD: 18! You're *old*!

JOSH: I married young.

BRAD: *Community* college! You're *poor*, too.

JOSH: He chose it, okay?

BRAD: My kid? One day, I'll be checking out Ivy League schools for him.

JOSH: If I were you, I'd start checking out *now*.

BRAD: Why?

JOSH: For all *you* know about him, he's already out of high school.

BRAD: Oh, yeah?

JOSH: Yeah!

BRAD: Oh, yeah?

JOSH: Yeah!

BRAD: *(Into his cell phone)* Hello, Sal? How ya' doin'?…Good… Good…Sal, it's your busy time, I know, so I'll get right to it. My boy's birthday next week – what? Sal, I didn't say *next* week, I said *last* week…Oh, *this* week…Look, I'll tell you what I want – what?…Yes, I'll wait.

JOSH: *(Into his cell phone)* Hello, Irv? How are you?…Great…Listen, I hate to call at this hour, Irv, but, as you know, my boy starts college in the fall and–

BRAD: *Community* college.

JOSH: *(Into his cell phone)* – the best community college on the East Coast. So, of course, he needs wheels… For a teen-ager? I was thinking in terms of – sure, I'll hang on.

BRAD: *(Into his cell phone)* Sal, I've *got* the money!…Sal, what are we talking here? A few bucks…Big Brad is *not* going to stick you like last time! A bounced check is not a federal crime, you know – I don't think I'll be deported!…Okay…Okay!…I was thinking of rollerblades, actually. The *trendy* ones, bells and whistles, you know? They're *in*, right?

JOSH: Rollerblades! You're poor!

BRAD: *(Into his cell phone)* The most expensive pair in the store, Sal! As long as they're *trendy!*

JOSH: *(Into his cell phone)* So, Irv, I'm thinking the Neon would do for him.

BRAD: Neon! Get him a cardboard box and be done with it!

Into his cell phone.

What *is* in this month, then?

JOSH: Calendars are in. You can put an "X" on his birth date, to help you remember it.

Into his cell phone.

Okay, *not* a Neon. What's your suggestion?

BRAD: *(Into his cell phone)* Sure, if mini-scooters are *trendy!*

JOSH: *(Into his cell phone)* Right! I was thinking of a Saturn myself, Irv!

BRAD: *(Looking at JOSH angrily, talking into his cell phone)* No! A mountain bike, Sal! The kid is ready for a mountain bike!

JOSH: *(Into his cell phone)* A Land Rover, what about a Land Rover? Those Brits know how to build 'em, right?

BRAD: *(Into his cell phone)* The finest mountain bike on the market!... What?...Well, *find* a mountain bike, Sal! Just make sure it's expensive!

JOSH: *(Toward BRAD'S phone)* And *trendy!*

Into his own cell phone.

A Cadillac is what I'm after, Irv...You heard me! Why go for less when you can afford more?

BRAD: *(Into his cell phone)* A Moped, that's what the kid ought to have. A Moped, you hear me?...What do you mean, you don't carry them?

JOSH: *(Standing as HE talks into his cell phone)* Better yet, a Lincoln Continental!...Vi? What *about* Vi?...*I* call the shots in my house!

BRAD: *(Standing as HE talks into his cell phone)* Better yet, a 3-wheel ATV. All-Terrain-Vehicle, *that's* the ticket. Why go for less when you can afford more?

JOSH: I *said* that already!

BRAD: I *thought* it first.

JOSH: *(Into his cell phone)* A Lexus, Irv! The kid deserves a Lexus!

BRAD: *(Into his cell phone)* I *know* he's only five, Sal! But that's close to six, which is close to seven!

JOSH: *(Into his cell phone)* Yes, I said Lexus!...So he's only 18, so what? He'll be 19 someday, won't he? He'll be 20 someday, won't he?

BRAD: *(Into his cell phone)* Then who *does* carry ATVs, Sal?... Because when his own brother gives big Brad a hard time, big Brad goes somewhere else, okay?

JOSH: *(Into his cell phone)* A Jaguar, why not!...If I say a Jaguar, I *mean* a Jaguar!...So I've upgraded a little, so what?

BRAD: *(Into his cell phone)* Better yet, I'm saying a Harley-Davidson! The kid's advanced for his age!

JOSH: *(Into his cell phone)* Sure, a BMW! Four-on-the-floor! Why the hell not!

Suddenly, LYDIA *reappears. This time,* SHE *turns her back to them and bends over, displaying a bit of buttock.* SHE *bows her head, brushes her long hair over her face, and secures it with a headband.*

All this stops JOSH *and* BRAD *cold.* THEY *stare, mesmerized, wondering what she'll do next.*

BRAD: *(Into his cell phone)* Hello, Sal? Later.

HE *puts away his cell phone.*

JOSH: *(Into his cell phone)* Hello, Irv? Goodbye.

HE *puts away his cell phone.*

What LYDIA *does next is spritz toilet water over the nape of her neck, and her arms.*

JOSH *and* BRAD'S *ensuing exchanges are perfunctory and non-combative, even robotic, as* THEY *watch* LYDIA, *who now spritzes toilet water on her bare waist.*

BRAD: It's expensive to maintain a BMW.

JOSH: No more expensive than maintaining an orthodontist.

BRAD: If it weren't crowded in the next car, I'd be out of here like a shot.

JOSH: If I could breathe away from this open door, I'd be gone in a second.

THEY *stare at* LYDIA. *A cell phone ring barely interrupts their respective reveries. Again,* THEY *hardly know what they're saying.*

BRAD: *(Quietly)* That's Vi. Irv called her. He told her you've gone bananas.

JOSH: *(Quietly)* It's old Janice. She's calling to tell big Brad he's off the wall.

BRAD: *(Quietly)* A BMW for a community college smart-ass. Vi is blowing her top.

JOSH: *(Quietly)* A Harley-Davidson for a boy who's 5 or 6 or 7. Old Janice will chew you up and spit you out.

Without taking his eyes off LYDIA, BRAD *holds out his cell phone to show it is not ringing. This forces* JOSH, *his eyes fixed on* LYDIA *the whole time, to answer his own cell phone.*

Into his cell phone.

Hello?...Vi, why do you bother me when I have work to do?...Who *says* I ordered a BMW?...It was a joke.

BRAD: *(Quietly)* What did I tell you.

JOSH: *(Into his cell phone, also quietly)* I swear it, a joke...Well, frankly, Vi, that brother of yours is a troublemaker!

Suddenly, BRAD'S *cell phone rings.*

Hah! Janice! Big Brad's in for it.

Into his cell phone.

What, Vi?...No, Vi, just this guy who –

LYDIA, *her ablutions over, playfully sends a toilet water spray in the direction of* JOSH *and* BRAD; *then* SHE *leaves the car.*

This brings JOSH *and* BRAD *back to their senses and to their competitiveness.*

BRAD: *(Into his cell phone)* Hello?

Triumphantly to JOSH.

It's Babycakes!

JOSH: Yeah, right!

Calling out in the direction of BRAD'S *cell phone.*

It's true, Janice! He's buying a–

BRAD *puts his cell phone to* JOSH'S *ear.*

He called Sal, I heard him, and – what?...Oh...Oh...How do you do, Babycakes?

HE *turns to his own call sheepishly.*

Nothing, Vi, nothing at all...This guy on the train – what?...No, he just introduced me to Babycakes, that's all...*Babycakes!* ... I can't

help it – that's her name…It's too complicated to explain…So how
are the kids?

BRAD: *(Into his cell phone)* Just this guy on the train…*Sweet*? If he *is*
sweet, I haven't noticed…He has this wife named Vi…Vi, as in–

To JOSH

Viola? Violette?

JOSH: Beatrice.

BRAD: Beatrice? *Beatrice*?

JOSH: She hates "Bea", so I call her "Vi".

BRAD: *(Into his cell phone)* Beatrice…It's too complicated to explain…
So what is it now, Babycakes? Last night wasn't enough?

JOSH: *(Into his cell phone)* I *never* met Babycakes before in my life! I
swear it! Where would *I* ever meet Babycakes?…What?…

BRAD: *(Into his cell phone)* You want what tonight? You want what
where tonight?…

To JOSH

This girl is a sex maniac!

HE *puts the cell phone to* JOSH'S *ear.*

JOSH, *albeit reluctantly, listens, his facial expressions registering
shocked interest.*

Suddenly, having heard enough, HE *pushes the phone back to* BRAD
and returns to his own call.

JOSH: *(Into his cell phone)* Vi, I am *not* acting funny. Why would I
be acting funny?

BRAD: *(Into his cell phone)* Babycakes, big Brad could have a *heart*
attack listening to you!

JOSH: *(Mistakenly into his own cell phone)* Then *don't* listen, idiot!…
No, not you, Vi. I listen to you. I always listen to you…

BRAD: *(Laughing into his cell phone)* You stop! You *stop* that! You
could get arrested for *thinking* that!

JOSH: *(In the direction of* BRAD'S *cell phone)* We're in a public place
here, Babycakes!

HE *puts his finger into his ear and tries to talk into his cell phone
at the same time.*

What?…Vi, why would I be behaving weirdly on a stalled train in
the summertime, for God's sakes?…Vi, I need to work, you hear
me? I–

Suddenly, LYDIA *reappears. This time, instead of cooling herself off at the end of the car,* SHE *begins a languorous walk toward* JOSH *and* BRAD.

BRAD: *(Into his cell phone)* Babycakes? I'll get back to you.

HE *exits his cell phone.*

JOSH: *(Into his cell phone)* Vi? I'll talk to you later.

HE *exits his cell phone.* HE *puts his pad and attaché case away.* HE *smoothes his hair over his bald spot.* HE *uses a breath spray.*

BRAD: You're being a bit "junior high" here, aren't you, fella?

JOSH: I'm being 44, fella.

BRAD: It's unnatural to be 44, fella!

JOSH: You'll find out soon enough, won't you, fella!

BRAD: Oh, yeah?

JOSH: Yeah!

BRAD: Oh, yeah?

JOSH: Yeah!

LYDIA: Excuse me, gentlemen. May I inquire about that middle seat? It isn't reserved?

JOSH *and* BRAD *shake their heads.*

The alternatives tonight seem to be (a) standing up in an air-conditioned car between several teenage octopi; and (b) sitting down in this hotbox between two civilized adults. Which shall it be, I wonder?

JOSH *and* BRAD, *still mesmerized, look at her without moving.*

The *second* alternative is the more promising, I think. Which of you owns the trendy footwear?

There is no response.

Which of you owns the stylish garment?

There is no response.

Shall I guess?

Handing the shoes to BRAD.

You for the excitingly "now" shoes, Mr. Young Hunk.

Handing the jacket to JOSH.

You for the dashingly classic jacket, Mr. Mature Honcho. Am I right?

JOSH: Yes.

HE *puts his jacket over the back of his seat.*

BRAD: Yes, indeed.

HE *puts on his shoes.*

There is a sudden movement of the train.

LYDIA: Moving, at last! A wonderful start for a joyous trio!

BRAD: Yes.

JOSH: Yes, indeed.

The train stops again abruptly.

LYDIA: Wrong! Stalled again!

SHE *is about to sit when the train lurches.* SHE *falls into* BRAD'S *lap.*

Oops! Shall I apologize?

Another lurch in the train and SHE *falls into* JOSH'S *lap.*

Oops! Shall I feign embarrassment?

Finally, SHE *makes it into the middle seat.*

There! If comparisons weren't odious, I'd confess which lap was the more stimulating. But my lips are sealed, and sealed shall remain.

Looking from one to the other.

It is *blazing* in here. I suspect, however, it is not the defective air-conditioning. No, I appear to be perched between the most *masterful* men I have ever encountered, their names unknown, even as they throw off their body heat!

To BRAD

Your name, Mr. Young Hunk?

BRAD: Mr. Brad. I mean, Brad.

LYDIA: So: the light-complected one, with the rippling pectorals easily identifiable beneath the snug shirt, is Brad. Not Brad Pitt, by a long shot, but a Brad is a Brad all the same, is he not?

BRAD: Yes.

LYDIA: *(To* JOSH*)* Is he not?

JOSH: Not always.

LYDIA: "Not always", declares Mr. Mature Honcho. Your name, please?

JOSH: Mr. Josh. I mean, Josh.

LYDIA: So: the darkish one, with the eyes burning bright, like a tiger in the night – the spitting image of Antonio Banderas, I might add – is

Josh. And the name, you ask, of the audacious creature sandwiched between you? My new friends, I am Lydia Lopatkin.

SHE *takes a fancy package of nuts from her shopping bag and holds it out to* JOSH.

Something I can give you, Josh?

JOSH: No, thank you.

LYDIA: *(To* BRAD*)* Something I can give you, Brad?

BRAD: Not in full view of my elders.

LYDIA: Why, Brad, I believe you are reaching for improprieties!

Taking one nut, SHE *puts the package away.*

I shall *ignore* that and tell you about my day. As a beginning but eager anthropology student at NYU, I *ought* to have spent it in the library, working on the article I intend to publish. Instead? Instead, this afternoon, I said to myself, "No, Lydia Loptakin, today you will try a new 'persona'! Today you will have adventures, wild, young, madcap adventures." Guess what I did, Josh?

JOSH: I can't.

LYDIA: You, Brad? Now, don't reach for improprieties again, unless you can't help it.

She shakes the shopping bag.

Would a clue be in order?

BRAD: You shopped.

JOSH: I was just going to say that!

LYDIA: Shopped, Mr. Young Hunk? Shopped, Mr. Mature Honcho? My new "persona" literally *propelled* me to Saks Fifth Avenue, paradise of whim and whimsy! First, the Gift Shop, to acquire that outrageously fattening assortment of nuts you saw. One might just as well apply them directly to one's hips! The hip brushing your own cannot possibly want augmentation, can it, Josh?

JOSH: Yes. No! I mean, I don't understand the question.

LYDIA: Brad?

BRAD: A few nuts couldn't possibly mar the hip brushing mine.

LYDIA: A very good answer, Brad. What did this mad girl do next? She strolled into the Lingerie Salon. And what, of all divine but senseless things, caught her wayward eye there? Can you imagine, Josh?

JOSH: I have no imagination. I do taxes.

LYDIA: Brad?

BRAD: A nightgown.

LYDIA: You peeked.

BRAD: I *didn't*. A see-through nightgown.

LYDIA: What color?

BRAD: Black.

JOSH: *(Quickly) I* was going to say black!

LYDIA: Since it is, actually, black-on-black, you are *both* correct, gentlemen. Do I need this divine but senseless thing? I do *not*. I never wear nightgowns in summer. Still, one should be a bad girl *sometimes*, shouldn't one?

JOSH & BRAD: *(Simultaneously)* Oh, yes!

LYDIA: Such enthusiasm! I may *never* get off this train! Nonetheless: sage advice is called for here. A girl can be bad and still be good, can she not? She may buy a nightgown, but, unlike a fallen virgin, undo the damage the next morning. *Shall* I return it? What do you think, Josh?

BRAD: *Don't* return it, no!

JOSH: *(To* BRAD*)* She's asking *me*!

To LYDIA

Go to the library *first* to finish your work – that's the important thing. Then, return it.

LYDIA: A very good answer, Josh. Still, it's not so easy. If I described the nightgown, perhaps you would understand the power of my impulsive urge.

BRAD: Describe it to *me*!

LYDIA: I'm in discussion with my friend, Josh, at the moment. You forget, Brad, how much he looks like Antonio Banderas.

To JOSH

As we've already established, it's black and see-through. *And* made of chiffonette. Do you know what chiffonette is?

BRAD: I know! I know!

JOSH: She's asking *me*.

BRAD: Do you know?

JOSH: It's a – fabric.

BRAD: *(Scornfully)* Well, duh! A fabric! What kind of answer is that?

JOSH: It's a fabric used for nightgowns!

BRAD: Hah!

To LYDIA

A smoother, softer version of chiffon which drapes better than chiffon itself.

LYDIA: That's quite remarkable, Brad.

BRAD: One of our copywriters put that in an ad once.

All proud smiles.

I'm in advertising.

LYDIA: Advertising. That is *fascinating.*

JOSH: *(Abruptly)* I know what flannel is!

BRAD: *(Scornfully)* Flannel! The best you come up with is *flannel*? Would Lydia Lopatkin care to be seen in–?

JOSH: If Lydia Lopatkin cares to be seen in flannel, she has every right to be seen in flannel!

LYDIA: Actually, I *have* a flannel nightgown.

JOSH: Hah!

BRAD: *(Dejectedly)* You do?

LYDIA: On some of our cooler nights? I curl up on my bed, all toasty, nothing touching my skin but soft, creamy flannel. You can imagine, I'm sure.

BRAD: *I* can imagine! *He* can't: he does taxes.

JOSH: Two seconds ago you couldn't even imagine a flannel nightgown!

LYDIA: Sometimes, I sleep restlessly. The thing will fall open to the waist. Can you imagine!

JOSH & BRAD: *(Simultaneously)* I can!

LYDIA: *(To* JOSH*)* How do you come to know about flannel, Josh?

JOSH: One of my clients – one of my more heavily taxed clients, I might add – is in basic textiles. I pick up things from him.

LYDIA: Really!

JOSH: Griege goods – that means unfinished goods – *and* dyed goods.

LYDIA: Greige goods and dyed goods *both.* That's *fascinating*!

BRAD: *I* have fascinating things to tell, too!

JOSH: I'm not finished telling *my* fascinating things!

To LYDIA

Would you be interested to know one of my all-time favorite fabrics?

LYDIA: I would be very interested to know, Josh.

BRAD: Polyester! He likes checked polyester!

JOSH: I *hate* polyester!

To LYDIA

Especially checked polyester.

LYDIA: I believe that, Josh. What *is* one of your all-time favorite fabrics, then?

JOSH: Corduroy.

LYDIA: Is it! It's one of my favorites, too!

JOSH: I have a corduroy jacket that's eleven years old. It's still a perfect fit.

BRAD: Size 48 portly, right?

LYDIA: *(To* BRAD*)* You *are* getting testy, Brad. I don't think *that* will do, do *you?*

To JOSH

Do you look masterful in your corduroy jacket, Josh? Don't be modest now.

JOSH: As a matter of fact, I do.

BRAD: My rippling pectorals are easily identifiable beneath my snug shirt, don't forget *that!*

JOSH: I never heard anything so dumb!

BRAD: No dumber than your eleven year old corduroy jacket!

LYDIA: *(To* BRAD*)* Hush, Mr. Young Hunk. In due time. In due time.

To JOSH

I can *see* you in that corduroy jacket, Josh. Leather patches at the elbows. Yes?

JOSH: *(Crestfallen)* No leather patches: I *am* sorry.

Brightening

They could be sewn on, couldn't they?

LYDIA: Many men arrange for that very thing.

BRAD: *(Rising and turning to show off his backside)* I've been told I have buns of steel.

LYDIA: Oh, I *have* left you out of the conversation too long, haven't I, Brad! I haven't meant to, honestly. Tell me *your* favorite fabrics.

BRAD: *(Clenching his buttocks)* A man with buns of steel doesn't *have* favorite fabrics.

LYDIA: But I thought I caught a certain glimmer in your eyes when I spoke of my flannel nightgown. Wasn't that a glimmer?

BRAD: It *was* a glimmer, as a matter of fact.

LYDIA: You find flannel sensuous, perhaps?

BRAD: It's not in the same league with *other* fabrics though, is it!

LYDIA: A valid point, I would say.

JOSH: *(Jealously)* Flannel *can* be sensuous. It can be *very* sensuous.

BRAD: She asked *me*, not you.

To LYDIA

This is how I see it–

Suddenly, a cell phone rings. JOSH *holds out his, to show it is not ringing.*

JOSH: Your cell phone's ringing, big Brad. It's probably Babycakes.

LYDIA: Who's Babycakes?

JOSH: Or even the Leggy One.

LYDIA: Who's the Leggy One?

JOSH: I would call them – hobbies of some sort.

BRAD: *(Scowling at* JOSH, HE *turns to whisper into his cell phone)* Hello?

With much relief.

Hi!

JOSH: Babycakes! Right?

BRAD: It's Mr. Bernard. My client, Mr. Bernard!

Into the cell phone.

How are you?

HE *gives the cell phone to* JOSH.

Care to verify?

JOSH: *(Pushing the phone aside)* Aggh.

BRAD: *(Into his cell phone)* What can I do for you, Mr. Bernard?... Oh, there must be some mistake. I *never* told Crystal to cancel my ticket...I *never* said that! What can be wrong with that girl?

JOSH: Aggh.

LYDIA: Is Mr. Bernard a young hunk like you, Brad?

BRAD: *(Hand over cell phone, and looking pointedly at* JOSH*)* He's the oldest client I have. He's 43.

Into his cell phone.

Why, my ticket is right here in my breast pocket!

JOSH: *(Toward* BRAD'S *phone)* He doesn't even *have* a breast pocket, Mr. Bernard!

BRAD: *(Into his cell phone)* Yes, I look forward to meeting Mrs. Bernard, too. Goodnight – and thanks for bringing this to my attention.

HE *exits his cell phone.*

I'll call my ticket broker in the morning. *He'll* fix it up.

LYDIA: That was masterfully handled, Brad.

BRAD: Big Brad handles *everything* masterfully.

JOSH: Aggh.

BRAD: Big Brad was, I believe, about to give his thoughts on flannel.

LYDIA: Yes, you were.

BRAD: Flannel is sensuous, yes, but it can't hold a candle to black-on-black, see-through chiffonette, you see?

LYDIA: A *very* good answer, Brad. Given those buns of steel, there would be *no* other favorites, I gather?

BRAD: Actually – I prefer *bare* skin.

JOSH: He's reaching for improprieties again, Lydia!

LYDIA: *Are* you reaching for improprieties again, Mr. Young Hunk? If you are, I forgive you, as long as you can't help it, and are subtle about it. Can you be subtle?

BRAD: I can be *very* subtle.

JOSH: Hah! Subtle like a charging hippopotamus!

LYDIA: Gentlemen, gentlemen! Fabrics seem no longer to offer serene conversational opportunities. Let us change the subject. I will start with a confession: the mad girl with the new "persona" did not enter this car accidentally. Oh, no! She surmised that more than camaraderie was available here. Oh, yes, she studied closely, *very* closely before she sat with you. Can you guess why? Brad? Josh?

JOSH *and* BRAD *shake their heads no.*

Why, my article, of course, the article which, as a beginning but eager anthropology student, obsessed with behavior of animal groups, I intend to publish. My article has a daring and provocative working title. Guess what that title *is*, Mr. Young Hunk?

BRAD: Let Josh go first.

JOSH: Why do *I* go first all the time?

LYDIA: That working title is – are you ready? – *A Young Scientist Looks at Horniness.*

BRAD: *(Taken somewhat aback)* Looks at–?

JOSH: *(Taken more than somewhat aback)* – Horniness?

LYDIA: Precisely! *Antlers!*

Demonstrating with her hands.

The fantastical display of wondrous antlers, graceful, intricate, fanciful, a flamboyant fretwork of horns! In short: Horniness! Daring? Provocative?

JOSH & BRAD: *(Simultaneously)* Provocative/Daring.

Exchanging adjectives.

Daring/Provocative.

LYDIA: I *knew* you'd respond well. I intuited, you see, that right here, in this car, wondrous antlers were being displayed – oh, only metaphorically speaking, of course. You do understand?

BRAD: *(Hiding puzzlement)* Perfectly.

JOSH: *(Feigning comprehension)* Could it be clearer?

LYDIA: My hypothesis is – you do know what a hypothesis is?

JOSH: *I* know, *I* know! It's that long side, in a triangle!

BRAD: Hah!

LYDIA: I'm afraid that's a hypotenuse, Josh.

BRAD: *(Standing ceremoniously)* A hypothesis is a tentative assumption made in order to test logical or empirical consequences.

HE *sits.*

LYDIA: That's *exceptional*, Brad. How do you come to know?

BRAD: Those nerdy types in the Media Department: *always* testing some hypothesis or other to explain a ratings decline.

JOSH: *(Quickly)* *I* know what a ratings decline is!

LYDIA: I'm sure you do, Josh, but we don't want to sidetrack the conversation, do we! My hypothesis relates to the Alpha Male in animal groups. Alpha, the first letter of the Greek alphabet, stands for the first in the group, the socially dominant animal, you see?

JOSH *and* BRAD *nod, but it is obvious* THEY *don't see.*

With his wondrous antlers on display, Mr. Alpha Male is easily recognizable among stags. But in the case of *metaphorical* antlers – you see?

JOSH *and* BRAD *nod, but it is obvious* THEY *don't see.*

Besides which, of course, Mr. Alpha Male doesn't reveal himself when solitary. Surely you know that?

JOSH *and* BRAD *nod, but it is obvious* THEY *don't know.*

A setting is required: at least one other male, spurring him to express dominance.

Gesturing to JOSH *and* BRAD.

You two, for ready example. *One* mighty stag is Mr. Alpha here, presenting his wondrous metaphorical antlers to the lesser stag.

Pointing to herself.

Presenting them as well to the female creature, who will try to exert a powerful stabilizing force. Isn't that fascinating? Irresistible?

JOSH & BRAD: *(Simultaneously)* Fascinating/Irresistible.

Exchanging adjectives.

Irresistible/Fascinating.

LYDIA: My article is a treatise on *real* antlers, of course. *Real* antlers have not one, but *two* purposes. The first purpose, gentlemen?

JOSH *and* BRAD *shrug:* THEY *don't know.*

Why, the fierceness of weaponry, naturally! The very presence of antlers invites head-to-head combat. To secure dominance, Mr. Alpha attacks the hapless other until there is a gesture of submission.

BRAD: He does?

JOSH: There is?

LYDIA: My, yes!

She acts out a gesture of submission.

But, you see, in the case of metaphorical antlers, such as *you* display… well, things become a bit more difficult. *Which* is the Alpha Male? *Which* is the hapless other? How to establish position in the absence of wondrous antlers? The non-existence of wondrous antlers? The situation becomes – well, obfuscated!

BRAD: *His* wondrous antlers are absent. *And* non-existent! And obfuscated!

JOSH: Obfuscated? Whose wondrous antlers are obfuscated?

LYDIA: Hush, Josh; hush, Brad. There is a second purpose for Mr. Stag's horniness, a more *lascivious* purpose, but – well, frankly, you make me reluctant to explore it.

JOSH: Don't be reluctant, Lydia!

BRAD: To hell with reluctance, Lydia!

Suddenly, JOSH'S *cell phone rings.*

To JOSH

Your cell phone's ringing, Josh. It's Vi.

To LYDIA

You and *I* will explore the second purpose of horniness!

JOSH: No! Wait for me! *I* want to explore horniness, too!

Into his cell phone.

Hello?

BRAD: Vi, Josh?

JOSH: Irv! It's Irv!

Into his cell phone.

Yes, Irv? What can I do for you this horny – I mean, this humid evening?

HE *laughs.*

Oh, that! A misunderstanding, Irv!...I did *not* say you were a troublemaker. You are not by any stretch of the imagination a troublemaker...Irv, I have too much respect for the Automotive Dealers Association *and* the Four-State Area ever, *ever* to say such a thing!...Irv, it's this hotbox of a car. This train just will *not* move!

A little jolt: the train moves.

BRAD: Actually, it *is* moving.

JOSH: You call this moving?

BRAD: Yes, I call this moving! Lydia, isn't this *moving*?

JOSH: Stop trying to be Mr. Alpha Male, okay?

Into his cell phone.

Not you, Irv...Some guy in this car, with obfuscated antlers!

BRAD *rises threateningly,* LYDIA *trying to coax him back into his seat.*

BRAD: Do you *hear* him?

LYDIA: It's my hypothesis before our eyes!

BRAD: I have the most unobfuscated antlers in town!

LYDIA: Do sit, Brad. The second purpose of horniness is, of course—

JOSH: *(Quickly, into his cell phone)* Hold on a minute, Irv.

HE *turns his rapt attention to* LYDIA.

It's only Irv, Lydia. Go on! Explore!

LYDIA: Well, if we must: the second purpose of horniness is as a fearsome, pardon the word, sexual display.

JOSH: Sexual display, you say?

BRAD: Let's hear it for sexual display!

LYDIA: *(Gesturing with her hands)* Those wondrous antlers! Oh, yes, the lascivious exhibition is true of the elk, the ram, the moose. But we'll stick with Mr. Mighty Stag's, pardon the word, sexual display, since he's so iconic. Or shouldn't we?

JOSH: *(Into his cell phone)* I said, hold on, Irv!

To LYDIA

Stick with Mr. Stag, by all means!

BRAD: No problemo with Mr. Stag!

LYDIA: You are a quick study, Brad! And you, Josh! Mr. Stag does not realize, of course, that there's always someone younger, someone stronger, someone better-endowed. A depressing fact of animal life, but fact, indeed!

BRAD: Fact, if ever there was one!

JOSH: Who could deny such factuality?

LYDIA: It's the, pardon the word, testes which regulate the horniness of the Mr. Stags, you see.

SHE *uses her hand expressively, indicating size, length, shape suggestively.*

The wondrous antlers start, of course, with a small nubbin. You *do* know about the small nubbin?

JOSH & BRAD: *(Simultaneously)* Yes/No.

Exchanging responses.

No/Yes.

LYDIA: The small nubbin: barely perceptible, minuscule, soft, velvety. But the small nubbin *will* grow. Oh, yes! It will grow into a solid bony core, going through many stages of hardiness. From the underdeveloped and rudimentary, to the short and stubby, to the mid-length, and finally, of course, to the knockout full-length that defines Mr. Alpha Male.

She looks to BRAD *for confirmation.*

BRAD: *(Snapping out of his hypnotized state)* Full-length does it every time!

JOSH: *(Also snapping out of it)* Way to go, Mr. Mighty Stag!

LYDIA: Those wondrous antlers are, after all, pardon the word, erotic ornaments, you see.

BRAD: And why shouldn't they be?

JOSH: Erotic ornaments, you say!

Into his cell phone.

No, not you, Irv!

Still in a trance, to LYDIA.

Erotic ornaments, you say!

Again, into his cell phone.

What?...We're talking wondrous antlers, Irv! Erotic ornaments! Don't you know anything?

HE *exits his cell phone and turns to* LYDIA.

Go on, Lydia! Erotic ornaments, you say?

BRAD: This does not concern you. You *have* none!

JOSH: What? I have erotic ornaments you never dreamed of!

BRAD: Hah! I am *absolutely* loaded with erotic ornaments!

JOSH: Oh, yeah?

BRAD: Yeah!

JOSH: Oh, yeah?

BRAD: Yeah!

LYDIA: *(Laughing)* You two, honestly! What a confusion you make! You can't *both* be Alpha Male. Which one *is* it?

JOSH & BRAD: *(Simultaneously)* Well, it's not *him*!

LYDIA: Puzzlement reigns absolutely! At first glance, one would lean toward *you*, Brad, the younger, the taller, Brazilian lizard shoes at their station, so to speak.

BRAD: Absolutely at their station!

LYDIA: Pectorals rippling madly!

BRAD: The buns of steel, don't forget *those*!

LYDIA: And yet–

JOSH: And yet what, Lydia? And yet what?

LYDIA: And yet, here's Josh, wise, experienced, a huge residue of unspoken instincts–

JOSH: You never *saw* such a huge residue!

LYDIA: Why else would he harbor those enormous black, Antonio Banderas eyes –

JOSH: I've harbored them for years!

LYDIA: – burning, burning bright, like a tiger in the night!

JOSH: They burn all the time, Lydia, all the time!

BRAD: He's near-sighted, that's all!

JOSH: Oh, yeah?

BRAD: Yeah!

JOSH: Oh, yeah?

BRAD: Yeah!

LYDIA: *(Suddenly standing)* Oh, dear!

BRAD: Oh, dear what, Lydia? Oh dear *what?*

LYDIA: These frank exchanges have brought on a strong corollary need.

BRAD: Any corollary need of yours is a corollary need of mine.

JOSH: Corollary needs are my tax specialty!

LYDIA: Oh, but this corollary need is personal, gentlemen. There was a lavatory at the far end of the next car, as I remember. Yes or no?

JOSH *and* BRAD *shrug –* THEY *do not know.*

I'll simply have to wiggle my way through that crowd for relief, won't I?

Ready to exit, SHE *suddenly wheels about.*

Mr. Young Hunk and Mr. Mature Honcho! I will ask you to wait for me a wee jiffy. Then we can continue this stimulating exchange! You will watch my youthful indiscretions for me, won't you?

SHE *puts her shopping bag on the middle seat and sashays out.*

JOSH *and* BRAD *watch her exit in a deep silence. Finally,* THEY *look at each other and begin to snicker. The snickers grow into mighty laughter.*

BRAD: Mr. Alpha Male!

JOSH: Mr. Mighty Stag!

BRAD: The flamboyant fretwork!

JOSH: The fierce weaponry!

BRAD: The, pardon the word, sexual display!

JOSH: Velvety nubbins!

A pause. Then.

JOSH & BRAD: *(Simultaneously)* Horniness!

The laughter subsides in gradual steps as JOSH and BRAD begin to reflect on the impact of LYDIA'S ditzy conversation.

BRAD: She *wants* it, you know.

JOSH: Oh, she *wants* it, all right.

BRAD: She's *asking* for it.

JOSH: She's *begging* for it.

Another reflective beat. Then, suddenly, BRAD straightens his tie and tightens his belt. JOSH combs his hair over his bald spot and uses his breath spray.

BRAD: What do you think *you're* doing?

JOSH: What do you think I *think* I'm doing?

BRAD: Again with the combs and sprays?

JOSH'S response is to spritz his breath spray at BRAD.

You don't imagine it's *you*?

JOSH: Who, then? *You*?

BRAD: Whose Brazilian lizard shoes are at the station?

JOSH: Who's masterful in the corduroy jacket with the leather patches?

BRAD: Your corduroy jacket *has* no leather patches.

JOSH: It *will* have!

BRAD: You're overlooking the rippling pectorals!

JOSH: You're forgetting the eyes, burning bright, like Antonio Banderas in the night!

BRAD: *(Turning his back and flexing his buttock muscles)* Has Antonio Banderas got these buns of steel? I don't think so.

JOSH: Those buns of steel aren't *available*. Marty's high-powered bash, remember?

BRAD: Seven pages of the limited partnership tax rules, remember?

JOSH: Babycakes expects you! Or is it the Leggy One?

BRAD: Vi worries about you at this very instant!

JOSH: That's different.

BRAD: What's different about it?

JOSH: 44: *that's* what's different about it.

BRAD: *Act* 44, then!

JOSH: I *am*, you idiot!

JOSH *and* BRAD *turn from each other, tucking shirts and smoothing wrinkles.*

BRAD: The whole time she talked about those wondrous antlers, her eyes were glued on me!

JOSH: My wondrous antlers are bigger than your wondrous antlers any day of the week!

BRAD: You don't *have* wondrous antlers! You don't even have metaphorical antlers!

JOSH: The metaphorical antlers I don't have are bigger than the metaphorical antlers you don't have!

BRAD: There is only one Mr. Alpha Male and that's *me*!

JOSH: Oh, yeah?

BRAD: Yeah!

JOSH: Oh, yeah?

BRAD: Yeah!

JOSH: Your nubbin is underdeveloped!

BRAD: Your nubbin is minuscule.

JOSH: Rudimentary!

BRAD: Barely perceptible!

JOSH: Short! Stubby! Totally *obfuscated*!

BRAD: That tears it!

HE *faces* JOSH.

Fierce weaponry at the ready, Mr. Mature Honcho!

JOSH: What fierce weaponry?

BRAD: *This* fierce weaponry!

HE *grabs his short compact umbrella.*

Antlers at the station!

JOSH: *(Grabbing his long ambassadorial umbrella)* At the ready!

BRAD: *(Shouting his war cry)* To the bitter end!

JOSH *and* BRAD, *in heated combat, use their umbrellas to lunge, strike, thrust, parry, crisscrossing the stage several times as* THEY *duel.* BRAD *forces* JOSH *to his seat, umbrella at his throat. In the mayhem,* JOSH'S *attaché case opens, and papers fly about.*

JOSH: Agghhh! Mr. Wesley's quarterly return!

HE *manages to escape, besting* BRAD, *umbrella at his heart.*

In the fray, BRAD'S *shoes fall off.*

BRAD: Agghhh! No!

Using an old ploy.

Here she comes!

JOSH *turns to look.* BRAD *now gets the upper hand and forces* JOSH *to the floor.*

Bow to Mr. Alpha, old man!

HE *"spears" the tax return on the floor with his umbrella and holds it up.*

JOSH: Never!

Newly energized, HE *lunges.*

BRAD: Yield, Mr. Mature Honcho, yield! I want your submission gesture, and I want it *now*!

But JOSH *manages to deflect* BRAD'S *umbrella point, with, of all things, his cell phone. This causes pain to* BRAD'S *hand.* HE *drops the umbrella and grasps his injured fingers.*

Ouch!

JOSH: *(Now with the upper hand)* Submission gesture? How about a *victory* march!

HE *picks up* BRAD'S *shoe.* HE *puts it on his umbrella tip and waves it around.*

BRAD: Aggh! My *shoe*! My Brazilian lizard shoe!

JOSH: *(Parading about)* Josh is #1. Josh is #1

BRAD *trips him and* HE *falls to the floor, hitting his head on the seat nearest him. This brings* JOSH *to his senses.*

Ow!...What...What am I...What am I *doing*?

BRAD: You're taking revenge on my shoe!

JOSH: I'm taking revenge on – ! On a – shoe???...I must be out of my mind.

BRAD: An innocent shoe that never did you any harm! You – you hapless other!

HE *grabs the shoe from* JOSH'S *umbrella and, sitting on the floor, puts it on.* HE *finds the other shoe and puts it on, too.*

JOSH: Yes! I am going out of my mind!

Still in a fog on the floor.

I don't *do* this. I have a wife. I have children. I won my high school Citizenship Medal.

To BRAD

Brad! I won my – I mean, what *am* I doing? Somebody has to behave rationally. It has to be *me*...No, Brad! It has to be *us*!

HE *sees* BRAD *trying to rise.*

Where are *you* going?

BRAD: An Alpha Male is on his way to establish position with the audacious creature in the other car.

JOSH: No! Forget it! Forget Alpha Males, Brad! There's always going to be someone younger, someone stronger! That's what Lydia said! Remember?

But BRAD *again tries to rise.* JOSH *pushes him down.* JOSH *finds his cell phone on the floor and dials.*

Stay there! *Stay* there!

HE *calls on his cell phone.*

Hello, Vi?... I won my high school Citizenship Medal, didn't I? ... Yes! I *knew* I did! Listen, Vi, as soon as we pull into the station...I don't *know* which station, *any* station, I'm getting off. I'll get a cab or something – what? ...

HE *sees* BRAD *trying to rise again.*

Stay, I said.

Into his cell phone.

What?...It's only this guy on the train....It's too complicated to explain.

From the other car emerges DIRK, *a newcomer, who has obviously met* LYDIA *there;* HE *is using her fan to cool his forehead.* JOSH *doesn't see him.*

DIRK: *(Approaching* BRAD*)* This car is a hotbox. Are you Josh?

BRAD *points to* JOSH.

What are you guys doing on the floor?

BRAD: What does it look like we're doing on the floor?

DIRK: Pilates?

BRAD: It's too complicated to explain.

DIRK: My name is Dirk. If he's Josh, *you're* Brad. Yes! There they are, just where they're supposed to be: the rippling pectorals!

JOSH: *(Into his cell phone)* Listen, Vi, the reason I called is: I want to *thank* you for a rational life!...I said–

DIRK *heads for the window seat.* BRAD *dives for it.*

BRAD: That's *my* seat now!

DIRK: My! Possessive, aren't we!

HE *shrugs and takes the aisle seat.*

How long have *you* known Lydia Lopatkin? We just met on the lavatory line. She had this strong corollary need.

BRAD: Can it.

DIRK: My! Irritable, too!

JOSH: *(Into his cell phone)* Sure, whatever you want...Good...And, Vi? Thanks again for...keeping me – you know, sort of grounded? And *realistic*!

HE *exits the cell phone.* HE *stands and sees* DIRK.

Who are you?

BRAD: He's Dirk.

DIRK: And you're Josh, eyes burning, burning bright, like–

JOSH: Can it.

DIRK: What *is* it with you two? You're behaving like the stags in Lydia's article. It's about ...

JOSH & BRAD: *(Simultaneously) Can* it!

DIRK: (HE *shrugs.* HE *pulls out his own cell phone)* Hello, is this Scott? Guess who?...That's right...Well, of course, I haven't called you before – you've been otherwise engaged, so to speak. Little birds tell me, however, that it's over between you and Connor. True, Scott?

JOSH: *(Gathering up his things from the floor)* Brad! Listen to me, please! Lydia Lopatkin is just a frightened and confused little girl, never mind all the brave talk about "personas" and madcap adventures. Point those lizard shoes in another direction, okay? Point them toward that *sensible* one, that Babycakes, okay?

HE *brushes himself off and sits in a seat across the aisle near the exit door.*

BRAD: It's the Leggy One who's sensible.

JOSH: Whomever.

DIRK: That's "whoever."

JOSH: Don't start with me, bud!

To BRAD

Call the Leggy One! Antlers or no antlers, you need a powerful stabilizing force in your life!

DIRK: *(To* BRAD*)* Funny he should mention antlers. Lydia's article is–

JOSH & BRAD: *(Simultaneously)* Can it!

JOSH: *Call* her, Brad. Do yourself a favor and *call* her!

BRAD: *(Thinking seriously, then dismissing* JOSH'S *advice,* HE *uses his cell phone)* Hi! It's me! Listen, there's no way we'll make Marty's high-powered bash...I *know*, I'm disappointed, too, but I *am* tired and...I know, Babycakes, but–

DIRK: *(Rolling his eyes to the heavens)* Babycakes!

JOSH: No, Brad, no! The Leggy One!

DIRK: *(Into his cell phone)* So, it's true, then?...Well, guess what? I'm out of my relationship, too, Scott...What?

HE *laughs.*

I *will* call you Scotty, yes!...Dinner is good...Candles are good... Fine wine? Heaven is before us!

HE *laughs.*

Make the reservation ...Sure I'll wait, Scotty!

BRAD: *(Rolling his eyes to the heavens. Then, into his cell phone)* I'm tired, I tell you! A quick burger is all I can manage!

DIRK: *(Under his breath)* McDonald's! Large fries and Diet Coke!

BRAD: *(Into his cell phone)* Chinese food, then! Who *cares*?

DIRK: Ah so! Egg Foo Yung!

BRAD: *(Annoyed with Babycakes and with* DIRK'S *competitiveness)* Babycakes, I am not *sore*!...The Outback then, who gives a–

DIRK: *(Under his breath)* Shrimp on the barbie and *everything*!

Into his cell phone.

What? Oh, this senior citizen next to me...35, I'd say.

Whispering

It's unnatural to be 35, don't you think?

JOSH: You see, Brad? You *see*?

BRAD: *(Looking right at* DIRK *as* HE *blasts into his cell phone)* I'm *full* of energy, Babycakes! It's back to the City, to The Four Seasons for dinner!

JOSH: No, Brad, no! You can't afford The Four Seasons!

DIRK: *(To* BRAD*)* It's true. You can't afford The Four Seasons.

BRAD: How do you know I can't afford The Four Seasons?

DIRK: Because *no one* can afford The Four Seasons.

JOSH: Use your head, Brad! You need a reservation a month in advance.

DIRK: It's true. You need a reservation a month in advance.

BRAD: I *have* a reservation a month in advance.

DIRK: Liar, liar, pants on fire!

BRAD: Fibber, fibber, lips like liver!

Into his cell phone.

What?...Babycakes, I am *not* acting nutsy!...I do *not* sound like a schmuck! I know how I sound, and I do *not* sound like a schmuck!... Forget it, then, forget it, okay?...You know what your trouble is, Babycakes? You are *not* a powerful stabilizing force!

HE *exits his cell phone.*

DIRK: *(Sniggering)* Babycakes! *Nobody* is named Babycakes!

JOSH: *(To* BRAD*)* Old Josh tips his fretwork to you, big Brad!

DIRK: *(To* JOSH*)* What does *that* mean?

JOSH: It's too complicated to explain.

DIRK: *(Shrugging,* HE *returns to his cell phone)* What?...Excellent, Scotty...Yes, I'll meet you there...Fine...Fine...*A bientot!*

HE *laughs and exits his cell phone.* HE *turns to* BRAD.

My ex-boyfriend was French. *"A bientot"* means–

BRAD: Will you go tug on your nubbin someplace else?

DIRK: *(To* JOSH*)* What does *that* mean?

JOSH: It's too–

DIRK: – complicated to explain! My, what a *contretemps* is here!

Now HE *sees* LYDIA *returning.*

La Belle Dame Sans Merci! Ici, en fin!

To BRAD

That's also French. It means–

BRAD: Aggh!

LYDIA: Mission accomplished!

Taking the middle seat.

Have we all met? Dirk, this Young Hunk is Brad. Brad, this Frisky Pup is Dirk. And there is my good friend Josh, all by himself near the exit door. We cannot *have* this, Mr. Mature Honcho!

SHE *rises and goes to sit by* JOSH.

JOSH: Lydia! Please, *please* don't do this! *Any* of it!

LYDIA: Why, any of *what*, Josh?

JOSH: Don't *do* madcap adventures!

LYDIA: But, Josh, being young is all about madcap adventures!

JOSH: *Listen* to me, Lydia! Listen! You mustn't leave yourself wide open to strangers on trains.

LYDIA: But, Josh–

JOSH: No! No! You have to be more cautious. Avoid situations you can't control.

LYDIA: But my new "persona"–

JOSH: Forget new "personas". They're poses, Lydia, only *poses* that lead to trouble!

LYDIA: Why, you show real concern, Josh. I will remember your words and analyze them thoroughly when I get home. And, after all, who knows? Tomorrow I may choose an altogether *different* "persona!"

The car lurches and starts to move.

A station at last! Saved! We are saved!

JOSH: Remember, Lydia, *please*!

As the door opens, to BRAD.

Remember, Brad, *please*! There's always someone younger, someone stronger! Call the Leggy One! Call her!

HE *exits. Then, holding the door open,* HE *pokes his head back into the car and addresses* LYDIA.

I wish I *did* look like Antonio Banderas. I never have and I never will.

HE *exits.*

DIRK: What's *that* all about?

LYDIA: *(Returning to the middle seat)* One had to be there, I'm afraid. Wouldn't you say one had to be there, Brad?

BRAD: *(In his own thoughts)* What?

LYDIA: Wouldn't you say one had to–

But BRAD *stares straight ahead.* HE *is processing* JOSH'S *admonition.*

You see, Dirk, a moment ago we witnessed a spontaneous test of my hypothesis, a classic encounter to establish the Alpha Male. Demonstrable, pardon the word, sexual dominance, a competition about, pardon the word, erotic ornaments. Isn't that correct, Brad? Now, don't reach for improprieties, unless you can't help it.

BRAD: What?

DIRK: She said don't reach for improprieties. Although, I, for one, didn't think someone *your* age *could* reach for–

BRAD: You are looking for an antler straight to the heart, fella!

DIRK: I wouldn't try it, fella. My ex-boyfriend taught me Karate. It won't be a pretty sight.

BRAD: Yeah?

DIRK: *Oui.*

BRAD: Oh, yeah?

DIRK: *Mais, oui!*

BRAD *and* DIRK *glare at each other. Finally,* BRAD *realizing there's always "someone younger, someone stronger," blinks.*

BRAD: (HE *uses his cell phone)* Hello? It's me...It's so late, I'm thinking we won't make Marty's high-powered bash at all...You don't mind?...You *really* don't mind?

LYDIA: *(Pulling the nuts from her bag)* Is there something I can give you, Dirk?

DIRK: *(Reaching for nuts)* Pistachios! I *adore* pistachios!

LYDIA: Why, I adore pistachios too, Dirk! Only one might just as well apply them directly to one's hips.

SHE *touches one hip.*

The hip brushing your own cannot possibly want augmentation, can it?

DIRK: I don't *do* hips, Lydia.

Looking into the shopping bag.

Hawaiian macadamia nuts! My absolute *favorite!*

LYDIA: Now that's quite remarkable, Dirk.

DIRK: What's remarkable about it?

LYDIA: They are my absolute favorite, too!

DIRK: Hawaii is home to the world's best macadamia nuts, did you know? On some of the cold winter nights we have? One can fall asleep on one's couch munching away on macadamia nuts.

LYDIA: A very masterful picture you paint, Dirk.

BRAD: *(Eyes to the ceiling; then into his cell phone)* Well, good! I've never cared much for Marty's bashes myself.

LYDIA: It's Babycakes, I think.

DIRK: He *did* Babycakes.

LYDIA: It's the Leggy One, then.

DIRK: I keep *hearing* about her.

LYDIA: Josh would vote for *her*, I know. He's a wise man, Dirk, worth listening to in certain matters.

DIRK: What certain matters?

LYDIA: It's too complicated to explain.

BRAD: *(Into his cell phone)* Sure, we can stay home and rest! You're the sensible one in this pair…Sure! Thursday night? Your family? Whoever you want!

DIRK: That's "whomever".

BRAD *shoots him an angry look*

LYDIA: *(Whispering to* DIRK*)* Never mind, Dirk. You were, I think, about to tell me another of your favorites among my expensive assortment. Just what do you think about this plump and juicy hazelnut, Mr. Frisky Pup?

LYDIA *continues her patter as* DIRK *continues to choose from the assortment.*

BRAD *continues to talk to the sensible one on his cell phone.*

THE CURTAIN FALLS
END OF PLAY

EMILY, ON HER GLIDER

a one-act play

production history:

Emily, On Her Glider was presented in a staged reading by Stageplays Theatre Company, on January 21, 2002, at Repertorio Español, in New York City. The play was presented as part of an evening of two one-act plays exploring issues of multiculturalism in our society. Stageplays Theatre Company produced the event in association with The Hispanic Organization of Latin Actors. The play was directed by Tom Ferriter, with Rob Rodriguez as the narrator and the following cast:

Mr. Holmeier .... Richard Kohn
Emily Holmeier .... Lisa Miller
Antonio ("Nino") .... Ken Mayo

In April 2008, this play was presented by Around The Block Theatre Arts Workgroup at the New York Public Library (Mulberry Street Branch), New York City. It was directed by Marlene McCoy with the following cast:

Mr. Holmeier .... Louis Vuolo
Emily Holmeier .... Elizabeth Kingsley
Antonio ("Nino") .... Michael Morris

setting:
A back yard lawn area.
There are one or two deck chairs. A two-seat glider has just been brought out and cater-cornered in the center of the stage. The cushions for the glider are not yet in place

time:
The time is 1920. An afternoon in May.

characters:
EMILY, almost 30
ANTONIO ("NINO"), her lover
MR. HOLMEIER, her father

notes about the characters:

Emily: EMILY likes "tableaux." She creates them for herself.

In this play, she creates one on the glider: she sits, straight and regal, hands clasped, head tilted slightly. She does this where indicated in the stage directions.

This is, of course, a defense mechanism for her. Unsure of her looks, uncertain of her place in town society, she takes comfort in her tableaux.

EMILY also likes words and uses at least three of them where one would be necessary. These create verbal tableaux, and are also a defense mechanism; she feels most at ease when she is being most verbal.

Antonio: ANTONIO resents the fact that EMILY is trying to force a "persona" on him. He does not want it and does not need it for his self-worth.

ANTONIO bursts into anger at EMILY when he senses the pressure she aims at him. Still, he is genuinely sorry about the hurt he must bring to her.

Mr. Holmeier: MR. HOLMEIER knows that his daughter is something of a misfit in town. He knows that her love affair is doomed, and is pained that he cannot get her to see it.

AT RISE: EMILY *dusts the arms of the glider frame.*

FATHER *enters, carrying the glider cushions.*

FATHER: You moved the glider, Emily.

EMILY: Just a little.

FATHER: *(Handing her the cushions)* You should have waited for me.

EMILY: Thank you, Father.

Placing the cushions.

I wanted to take advantage of the lilac bushes. See the pretty corner it makes?

FATHER: You might have hurt yourself.

EMILY: But I didn't.

Laughing

Well…the cost does include one fingernail.

Looking at her watch.

Goodness, it's almost 4 o'clock.

FATHER: When will Antonio be coming?

EMILY: Well, that is a good question! His call was very mysterious. "I can't stay for dinner, but it is important I see you this afternoon."

Laughing

It's not like my Nino to be mysterious, is it!

FATHER: I don't know him well enough to say, I guess.

EMILY: Shall I tell you what I think is so important this afternoon? Or shall I keep it to myself?

FATHER: *(Warily)* You're getting your hopes up high, Emily. I worry when you get them so high.

EMILY: Do I do that?

FATHER: Sometimes.

EMILY: It depends, I suppose, on what one means by "so high."

A beat

My most favorite harbinger of Spring is, I think, taking the glider out of the musty shed. I keep this picture in mind all winter.

SHE *creates her tableau.*

There! Do I look pretty, sitting here like this?

FATHER: You always look pretty.

EMILY: Especially pretty?

FATHER: Especially pretty.

EMILY: *(Laughing)* Why go to the trouble, I ask myself! Nino will come straight from that smelly garage, overalls greasy, fingernails crusty!

FATHER: We mustn't fault the man on his work, Emily.

EMILY: I do!

Laughing

Oh, I know it's his work right now. Only–

A beat

I have a cheeky question for you, Father. Did Mother have trouble – forgive the word! – "civilizing" you?

FATHER: I came in from the railroad yard in greasy overalls, too.

EMILY: I know! That's why I ask!

FATHER: Your mother always had two large basins of hot water at the ready in the front hall.

EMILY: *(Smiling)* I remember those basins.

FATHER: It didn't bother me. She liked her house spotless.

EMILY: I remember that, too.

A beat

I don't do it nearly as well.

FATHER: Well enough for the two of us.

EMILY: Thank you, Father.

A beat

If it should turn out, Father, that you have to do for yourself from now on? If the right conversation takes place on this glider this afternoon?

FATHER: Then you are getting your hopes up high.

EMILY: On the contrary, I'm being realistic.

FATHER: Antonio doesn't strike me as a person who's ready to settle down, Emily.

EMILY: I can't imagine why you would say that.

FATHER: A young man of his background. Of his nationality–

EMILY: How little you know about us, Father! Neither background nor nationality enters into it when love is the issue!

FATHER: *(Blurting it out)* Emily, do you know Charley Harris? At the county clerk's office?

EMILY: Well, I guess I do. The most obvious man, Mr. Harris, descending on the Herbert and McCann Insurance Company minutes before I close the door, after some vital piece of information!

Laughing

That's what I'm to think, of course. It's his way of flirting.

FATHER: I ran into him this morning. He had a bit of news. Two bits of news.

EMILY: A man of his age, flirting!

FATHER: The first was about the garage where Antonio works.

EMILY: *(Listening at last)* Cathcart's Garage? What about it?

FATHER: Mr. Cathcart is going to move the business out of town and out of state.

EMILY: You mean, sell it?

FATHER: Charley Harris knows you've been seeing Antonio, and–

EMILY: I have not been seeing Antonio. My Nino has been seeing me. And Mr. Charley Harris is, obviously, envious of those attentions!

FATHER: But if Cathcart's Garage is leaving, what will Antonio do?

EMILY: What will he do? He will act. My Nino is ambitious and adventurous and enterprising. It won't surprise me to learn he is buying that garage himself! That's probably it, Father–

FATHER: No, Emily.

EMILY: I'll be the wife of a successful entrepreneur, a successful American entrepreneur!

Standing and laughing.

Oh! Now I've gone and told you what I think is so important about this afternoon's visit. So much for keeping it to myself!

FATHER: Your hopes are up very high then, Emily.

EMILY: Do they seem so very high to you? They don't to me. A woman of thirty–

FATHER: Twenty-nine.

EMILY: And you will forgo reminding me that my Nino is only–

FATHER: I don't want to see you hurt, Emily.

EMILY: Oh, I have thought, sometimes in the past, that a six year difference can be an impediment. But lately I've begun to understand that there is no impediment, none whatsoever. You may not have noticed, Father, but I have been changing. I have been changing before your eyes!

FATHER: *(Blurting it out)* Antonio has been seen in town with another girl, Emily. That was the other bit of news Charley had for me.

EMILY: *(Laughing)* Mr. Charley Harris is more taken with me than I thought! Nino does that, Father, makes sure he is seen in town with other girls. This is how the game is played these days.

FATHER: The girl he's been seen with, Emily, is–

EMILY: The girl he's been seen with is Marie Cathcart.

FATHER: Yes.

EMILY: The boss's daughter.

FATHER: Yes.

EMILY: Well, of course, he's been seen with Marie Cathcart! As if I didn't know! Marie is fat and unpopular and Mr. Cathcart doesn't begin to know what to do with her. My Nino walks with her sometimes, so she won't feel like the pariah she is! She's such a silly thing, Father, hanging around my Nino like a foolish dreamer. He can't very well chase her off, can he? Mr. Cathcart is his employer! Besides, she's far too young for Nino–

FATHER: The girl is nearly out of high school.

EMILY: –far too immature, far too shallow! Oh, yes, Nino tells me about her. Just as I tell him about the gentleman other than Charley Harris who envies his attention to me.

FATHER: You haven't mentioned him.

EMILY: Haven't I? The man from the Book Club? He seeks me out everywhere, to talk about the new literature, the novels of Booth Tarkington, which he admires inordinately! So you see? We are completely honest with each other. And we know each other so well!

Feigning secretiveness.

Of course, I haven't told my Nino that Mr. Tarkington's #1 fan is short and bald and very married! This is how the game is played these days!

FATHER: These are not wise things, Emily.

EMILY: We don't have to be wise: we're young! That's where I've changed, Father. A young woman of twenty-nine doesn't need to have that firm a grasp of things, I've discovered. Oh, I know that *everybody* thinks of Emily Holmeier as a person of total practicality, looking life squarely in the eye all the time! They never see the other side of me, the one with aspirations, all kept deep within me! When I began to work for Herbert and McCann, I imagined that a tall man in an understated jacket would come in one day, a teacher of English Common Law at the University. And he would ask me some arcane question…about insurance law and I would know the answer, I would help him with it and we'd talk about it, and then–

Laughing

But there has only been Charley Harris, forcing his way in minutes before closing. And the short, bald and very married man who wants to talk about the works of Booth Tarkington. And I began to think, "It's time to put my aspirations aside". But it's so hard, Father, because I also began to think, "My word: is it all over for me?" But it isn't. It isn't! I am loved by an honorable man who works in a garage! That's a grand thing, a very grand thing!

FATHER *stares at her glumly, his pain palpable.* HE *doesn't know what to do or say to help her.*

Don't look so glum, Father! My Nino is also a man who is on to important truths about the times we live in, knowing where the future lies, in industry, in machinery and speed, in progress, in moving forward. A man like my Nino, who wears greasy overalls but can be civilized with two basins of hot water will do nicely, thank you!

ANTONIO: *(Offstage)* Hello? Are you in?

EMILY: *(Calling)* We're out back, Nino!

Whispering to FATHER.

No more dreaming about professors of English Common Law from the University. I have changed. I have really changed!

ANTONIO *enters. Surprisingly,* HE *is not in overalls, but* HE *is well-dressed in suit and tie.* HE *carries one or two books and a small bouquet of flowers.*

ANTONIO: Emily. Mr. Holmeier.

FATHER: *(Shaking hands)* How are you, Antonio?

ANTONIO: Fine, Mr. Holmeier. Just fine.

Handing the bouquet to EMILY.

These are for you, Emily.

EMILY: Thank you, Nino. Aren't they lovely! And don't you look nice!

ANTONIO: I went home and put on my suit.

EMILY: You have certainly done that!

To FATHER

We must get these flowers into water this instant, Father.

FATHER: I'll do that, yes.

Exiting, to ANTONIO.

It was good to see you, Antonio.

EMILY: *(Calling after* FATHER*)* And maybe you won't mind getting us some berry crush?

To ANTONIO

I made us a huge pitcher.

ANTONIO: I am not a bit thirsty. It was hot and I stopped for a drink first.

EMILY: *(Calling after* FATHER*)* Later, Father!

To ANTONIO

Did you ever see a man leave a scene so quickly and so tactfully? What does he think is going to transpire here?

EMILY *pulls at* ANTONIO *and tries to kiss him.* HE *pushes her off as gently as possible.*

ANTONIO: No, Emily. Not with him inside.

EMILY: That never stopped you before.

ANTONIO: Still.

ANTONIO *moves away.* EMILY *realizes she may have been too forward, and pulls back.*

EMILY: *(Sitting)* It's grand that you'd go home and put on a suit for me.

ANTONIO: *(Holding out his hands to show dirty fingernails)* I didn't have time to shower.

EMILY: Do you think a bit of dirt under the fingernails will keep my young man from my glider?

SHE *rubs her hands in the dirt at her feet.*

There! Equals! We'll sit as equals. We'll talk as equals because we are equals!

SHE *makes room for him on the glider.*

Do I seem impulsive to you? Every girl has the right to be impulsive. What do you think?

ANTONIO: *(Evasively)* Everyone has the right to be whatever they want.

EMILY: Well said, my Nino.

ANTONIO: *(Uneasily)* I'm sorry to push myself on you like this. I know you have Book Club on Saturday afternoon.

EMILY: I've stopped going to Book Club, Nino.

ANTONIO: No! Why?

EMILY: It's not worth the telling.

ANTONIO: I want to hear.

EMILY: Oh…I had a run-in with the Club president, that's all. She said something – well, you don't want to know what it was, I'm sure.

ANTONIO: *(Showing his own insecurity)* A bad thing? About me?

EMILY: About me. She said I dominated the discussions and interrupted the conversations. I don't do that.

ANTONIO: Of course, you don't.

EMILY: I don't *think* I do that! We never really know ourselves, do we?

ANTONIO: You're right. We don't.

HE *goes silent.*

EMILY: I'll punish the Club for a month, until they see they can't do without my contributions. Isn't that a good idea?

ANTONIO: *(Handing her the books)* I'm returning your books, Emily.

EMILY: Goodness! I'd forgotten about them.

ANTONIO: I've kept them a long time. There's just been no time.

HE *goes silent again.*

EMILY: Is something wrong?

ANTONIO: No. Nothing's wrong.

EMILY: *(A beat)* I must say I found your call today a bit nervous-making. I mean: why aren't you at work at this very moment? Why aren't you there using those strong hands of yours, making piles and piles of money for us?

ANTONIO: I – I'm on leave. "Extended paid leave," he called it, Mr. Cathcart.

EMILY: You are!

ANTONIO: As of today.

EMILY: As of today!

ANTONIO: As of 3 o'clock today.

EMILY: But what in the world for?

ANTONIO: He's selling the garage. He's moving away.

EMILY: It's true then. I'm sure Mr. Cathcart has a reason, but it doesn't seem he could have a good reason, does it, Nino?

ANTONIO: He called me into his office and told me. That's all I know.

EMILY: But how short-sighted! Not to appreciate what he's giving up here? The only garage for miles and miles around? When the automobile is ready to take over beyond our comprehension? The pivotal years for autos looming just ahead, every street about to fill up with them, as though this town were some huge Eastern metropolis? Oh, yes, my Nino! The automotive arts are going to explode around us. I know that!

ANTONIO: *(Suddenly and jarringly furious with her)* Emily, why do you do that?

EMILY: Why do I do what?

ANTONIO: Pretend things. Make up things. Make fancy speeches! The "automotive arts!" There is no such thing.

EMILY: But there will be. I read about it at the office, all the time. Automobiles will become vastly more important to us, change our entire country, unite us!

ANTONIO: "Automotive arts!" That's so stupid!

EMILY: It's not stupid. It's a grand way to express what you're part of! Do you know, my Nino, that the word "garage" comes from a French word, a beautiful word, "garer." It means–

ANTONIO: *(Very scornfully)* Who cares about a French word! A small garage in a small town. Why act like it's anything more?

EMILY: *(Putting her hand over* ANTONIO'S *mouth)* We will not deny our futures, my Nino! The twenties are the era of expectation, and the automobile will fulfill the expectation. Any intelligent and adventurous and enterprising person can see. And I can guess that a certain intelligent and adventurous and enterprising person in a becoming business suit is about to make an announcement concerning the Cathcart garage.

ANTONIO: Stop, Emily! Stop!

EMILY: You're going to buy the garage. Am I right?

ANTONIO: Buy it!

EMILY: Yes, buy it!

ANTONIO: *(A beat:* SHE *defies belief)* You don't have an inkling, do you!

EMILY: An inkling of what?

ANTONIO: "Extended paid leave" means I'll be joining Mr. Cathcart later. When he finds his new place, I'll work for him again.

EMILY: Work for him again?

ANTONIO: Of course.

EMILY: But where?

ANTONIO: Wherever he goes.

EMILY: But why, when you could buy–

ANTONIO: Why? WHY?

Standing, getting angry again.

Buy the garage! What's wrong with you? What would give you an idea like that?

EMILY: Because, knowing you as I do–

ANTONIO: You don't know me! You don't want to know me! Buy the garage! If I wanted to, which I don't, where would I get the money?

EMILY: *(Not listening)* But don't you see? You would do the office work, my Nino. You would run things from behind a huge desk!

ANTONIO: Behind a desk!

EMILY: Yes! When you're the owner, Nino, when you are the entrepreneur, you won't have to crawl on your back under the car any more. You'd be at the telephone, ordering supplies, wearing starched white collars all day, hiring people, firing them. And your nails–

ANTONIO: No. No, Emily!

EMILY: No?

ANTONIO: *(Calmly, but sternly)* I like crawling on my back under the cars. That's where I am what I want to be!

EMILY: Nino, we are at the right point of beginning our lives afresh. You are in the right house, in the right yard, sitting on the right glider. Because you see, your Emily has saved a bit through the years, looking for just the opportunity to participate in bold, new directions, in–

ANTONIO: *(Grabbing her, his patience at the end)* Emily! Look at me! I can't add numbers without counting on my fingers! No, look at me! I can't read. I can not read! Mr. Cathart reads the instruction manuals aloud to me, so I can figure out what I am supposed to do! You see? You see?

EMILY: *(A beat. Then, quietly)* That isn't true, Nino. How can it be true? We met at the Book Club. A man doesn't join Book Club if–

ANTONIO: I thought they would help me learn to read. They didn't. I dropped out after three afternoons. Don't you remember?

EMILY: Four.

ANTONIO: Four afternoons. I hated those afternoons. I hated that phony talk about artists and poets – I felt stupid. You made me feel stupid, all of you! I'm not stupid!

EMILY: Of course, you're not stupid.

ANTONIO: *(In intense pain now)* Maybe I can't read. That doesn't make me stupid!

EMILY: Of course, it doesn't.

ANTONIO: Why wouldn't I stop going!

EMILY: *(Not sarcastically)* You didn't stop coming here, though.

ANTONIO: No. I didn't stop coming here.

EMILY: You didn't stop talking about books with me.

ANTONIO: No, Emily. You talked about books. I listened. No. I pretended to listen.

EMILY: I never noticed that.

ANTONIO: You never notice what you don't want to notice!

EMILY: I don't think that's true.

Becoming brave again.

Still, that didn't stop you from doing what you did afterwards.

ANTONIO: What we did afterwards.

EMILY: What we did afterwards. You liked that part of it.

ANTONIO: I loved that part of it.

EMILY: Then, you see? We love each other. So, whatever else may be, you're in the right house, in the right yard, sitting on the–

ANTONIO: I love that part of it with every girl I know, Emily.

EMILY: Nino?

ANTONIO: With every girl I know.

EMILY: I don't understand.

ANTONIO: You don't want to understand.

EMILY: I do want to understand.

ANTONIO: It doesn't mean I love every girl I know. I don't love any of them.

EMILY: Nino?

ANTONIO: *(Abruptly and firmly)* I'm going to get married, Emily.

EMILY: What?

ANTONIO: I'm going to marry Marie Cathcart.

EMILY: What?

ANTONIO: She's going to have my baby. In the Fall.

EMILY: Your baby?

ANTONIO: Mr. Cathcart will help us. He's going to find a house for all of us. He wants us to live with him. You see?

EMILY: I'm afraid I don't see.

ANTONIO: In a new place, in a bigger town, where no one knows us. We'll start again. All of us. You see?

There is no response.

I don't know if I love her. Maybe I do. I – I came here today to tell you, that's all. I owe it to you.

EMILY: *(Ready to hurt him now)* To me? And not to all those other girls, the ones who love that part of it with you?

ANTONIO: Don't do this, Emily.

Gently putting his hand over her mouth.

I owe it to you.

EMILY: Why? Why to me?

ANTONIO: Because you're different.

EMILY: How am I different?

ANTONIO: You feel things so oddly. You feel things so deeply. You get hurt so easily.

EMILY: I do? I don't think so at all.

A small wry laugh.

Goodness! How unnecessarily reticent Father is being! We may never get our berry crush!

ANTONIO: It's something I have to do, Emily. For Marie and for Mr. Cathcart.

EMILY: I suspect poor Father thinks we want to be alone, saying life-altering things to each other. But we don't want to, do we!

ANTONIO: Marie is my age, Emily.

EMILY: Your age.

ANTONIO: You're not old, Emily. I don't mean that.

EMILY: Of course, I'm not old!

Turning toward him.

Why, you think you know me so well, Antonio! You don't know me! Are you under the impression that I wanted to marry you?

Laughing

What a foolish young man you are! Smug and self-satisfied, far too young man! You are not the only person in this town who enjoys love affairs, Antonio!

ANTONIO: I want you to forgive me.

EMILY: Shall I remind you of the gentleman, the very worthy and mature gentleman who likes to talk to me about the books of Booth Tarkington?

ANTONIO: Please: I need you to forgive me.

EMILY: Oh, Mr. Tarkington is, as I've told you, just his excuse – you must understand, or can you? – to engage my attention. Still, I must tell you how refreshing it is to talk, really talk with a man about books, an educated man, a literate man!

ANTONIO: I'm glad that you've found someone, Emily. I am.

EMILY: What did you come here for, Antonio? My permission to go off with your young Marie Cathcart? You have that permission!

ANTONIO: I am sorry, Emily.

ANTONIO *tries to hug her, but* SHE *turns away.*

EMILY: Emily Holmeier marry a man who works in a garage? Who crawls under leaky automobiles every day? While someone reads instructions aloud to him? Marry a man who can never get the dirt out of his fingernails?

In an effort to stop EMILY, ANTONIO *puts his arms around her tenderly.*

SHE *calls out*

We are ready for cooling drinks out here, Father!

ANTONIO: But I am sorry. Please know that. Please!

ANTONIO *kisses her passionately.* EMILY *remains unmoved.*

EMILY: You're getting me dirty, Antonio.

ANTONIO *moves from her, looks at her a long time, and exits abruptly.*

EMILY *sits on the glider and rocks gently.*

FATHER *enters with three glasses on a tray.*

Only two glasses are required here, Father.

FATHER: Antonio?

EMILY: Antonio has left.

FATHER: So soon?

EMILY: Antonio has left because I have sent him away. That shouldn't prevent us from enjoying drinks on our glider, should it?

SHE *takes a glass.*

Thank you.

FATHER: Are you all right?

EMILY: I am fine.

FATHER: *(A beat)* He will be back? Emily?

EMILY: I'll be taking care of our house for a while longer, Father. Is that all right?

FATHER: Your home is here.

EMILY: It is, isn't it! I do have a home here, don't I?

FATHER: What has happened in this yard this afternoon?

EMILY: Don't look so glum, Father. Everything is just as it was this morning. Not every woman is old-fashioned, you see, like Mother. Not every woman is willing to take the time to "civilize" a man. A new age beckons us, Father: some men will be ready for it, and some men will not be.

FATHER: I tried to tell you, Emily. I tried to warn you.

EMILY: *(Laughing)* Two large basins of water in the front hall! Indeed! This is 1920. 1920! A woman who works in an insurance office and attends Book Club regularly has an infinite number of things to think about, a feast of possibilities. Any day now, a tall, well-dressed man may come into Herbert and McCann, a teacher of English Common Law, with some arcane question only I can answer for him.

SHE *touches the cushion.*

My most favorite harbinger of Spring is, I think, taking the glider out of that musty shed. I keep this picture in mind all winter.

SHE *begins her new tableau.*

You wouldn't mind if I don't have dinner with you just now, would you?

FATHER: We'll wait for dinner.

EMILY: Oh, no, you must eat! I want you to! I would like to sit here and swing by myself for a while. I do love it so, in front of the lilac bushes, swinging gently, reading my book. Do I look pretty, sitting here like this?

FATHER: You always look pretty.

EMILY: Especially pretty?

FATHER: Especially pretty.

EMILY: Thank you, Father.

Looking sadly back at EMILY, FATHER *exits.*

EMILY *opens her book.* SHE *cannot read at all.* SHE *swings gently in the glider, looking straight ahead.*

THE CURTAIN FALLS
END OF PLAY

MISS MONROE EXPLAINS

a dramatic monologue

Miss Monroe Explains

setting:
Interior of a small bedroom in a Brentwood cottage, dominated by an unmade double bed. A somewhat antiquated reel-to-reel tape recorder is the other prop necessary.

time:
Very late at night, some 45 or so years ago.

character:
MISS MONROE, about 35 years of age.

AT RISE: The stage is dark. The sound of a slamming door is heard, followed by the angry explosions of a female voice.

MISS MONROE:

Still in the dark.

Come back here, you hear, or I'll have your fucking head! This thing better work, you hear?

SHE *approaches center stage, still in the dark, muttering softly.*

Jerk! Idiot! Pricky gofer!

Into the machine.

Testing, one, two, three. Hello?

The spotlight comes up on the reel-to-reel tape recorder on the bed. Now the light takes in the blonde curls. Holding the microphone, MISS MONROE *raises her bent head, a shy half-smile on the sensuous mouth.*

Do you know me?

SHE *laughs shyly.*

I mean, my *voice*? Of course, you do! Still – I can't help worrying a little, you know? I mean, what if you *don't* remember me? What if, a year from now or ten years from now, you do *not* remember? Or care?

The light pulls back, revealing a drink in her hand.

I'm no good with these mechanical things, you know? I asked that whatever-his-name-is-pricky-gofer from the studio to set it up for me. Boy! He was out of here like a shot, so damned afraid of the studio! Why are people like that? If this *doesn't* work, I'll have his ass! One telephone call from me and he's out! *Out!*

A beat

Maybe not. Maybe it's not true any more now.

SHE *looks about. Her concentration is easily broken by unseen, unheard voices, or demons, or both;* SHE *goes out of the present and into the past easily.*

Have I eaten? I don't remember. I should eat something, toast or something, I guess. I can't. I just *can't*. That happens sometimes, if I'm nervous or frightened. Like when it was all happening, those movies one after the other, those actors getting sore at me, those moody directors yelling at me sometimes.

SHE *giggles.*

Sometimes? *All* the time!

A beat. SHE *sips her drink.*

Well, *that* won't happen any more, now that that cunt of a studio–

SHE *giggles.*

– oops! Pardon me. That word slipped out. Now that that–

A beat as SHE *finds the word.*

– *august* studio fired me, ordered me off the lot, no less. Me. *Me!* What do you think of that?

A beat

Recognize the dress?

The spotlight pulls back to reveal the pink satin dress SHE *is wearing.*

Ooh! I forgot: you can't see me. Well – you know the dress, *that* dress from – what was that picture called? It doesn't matter. When they canned me? I ran right over to the Wardrobe Department and took it. Why not? Why the hell not? It's mine, isn't it? Fucking A-right! I made the dress, didn't I? Fucking A-right! Not actually sewed it – some pricky gofer actually sewed it – but you know what I mean.

SHE *touches her breasts.*

These made the dress, right?

A beat

I figure you're picturing me in it, having a real show in your head, maybe, yes? Sort of remembering me the way I was when it was all happening, yes? That's not such a bad thing, is it?

SHE *sits on the bed. A long beat as* SHE *becomes increasingly forgetful of the microphone and the mechanics of recording, insuring that no tape will ever be made.*

I thought, if you don't mind, I'd call this tape "Miss Monroe Explains," because that's what I'll be doing, you see?

A beat

No. I *won't* explain about them firing me. Why should I? I don't care anymore. There are more important things to explain.

Her thoughts are miles away.

What was I going to say? I do that lately, forget what I was going to say. Why, I wonder.

Recovering her thoughts.

Oh, yes! I will tell you my *secret!* I will explain, really *explain*, because they don't understand, none of them, not that cunt of a studio, not those reporters, not those TV idiots, no one!

SHE *sips her drink.*

I will tell you what I never told my psychiatrists, what do you think of that? I had four psychiatrists, you know? Four different ones! Four psychiatrists, three husbands: lucky seven!

SHE *tries to hold up the appropriate number of fingers, but* SHE *cannot.* SHE *giggles.*

I never told my secret to Joe – you know the Joe I mean. I never told it to Arthur – you know the Arthur I mean, too.

A beat

You want to hear something crummy? Once, I called Arthur "Artie" and he threw a fit, right there on his parents' lawn! I went back to "Arthur" like a shot! But can you imagine? That you can't give your own husband a nickname? Why are people like that?

A beat

What I'm going to tell you? I *did* try to tell my first husband. His name was – I have trouble with names lately. Why, I wonder. He was nice. Quiet. Kind, sort of. So I thought, "Why *not* tell him?" That's what marriage is, right? A person you tell things to?

A beat

Only – I lost my nerve. I only told *half* the secret: that I wanted to be a star. I could *not* tell the other half, *why* I wanted to be a star.

A beat

I want somebody to know. *You*, out there! Why not? It isn't happening any more, is it? Being the star, making the movies and everything? I *want* to tell, because they don't understand, none of them, they – I said that already, didn't I?

A beat

You won't laugh at me, will you? Promise you won't laugh?

SHE *leans closer into the recorder.*

I have to tell my secret now, because I have this feeling, I just keep *having* it, that I'm, you know, not going to live much longer. Why, I wonder. It's just there, this feeling that some night I'll go to sleep and not wake up. Poof! Gone!

SHE *giggles.*

Probably with a phone in my hand! I make these calls at night, you know? Especially to – no, I am *not* going to tell you that! That is *not* the secret under discussion! Okay! Okay! I'm ready – the truth, the whole truth, nothing but the truth, like in those trial scenes. I wanted to be a star because...because...did you ever notice, in those movies, those *old* movies, the ones I went to, the ones you see late at night on TV? Beautiful clothes, hair and eyebrows and lips just so? Most of all, the apartments! I *loved* the apartments. White, all white! White bedrooms, white bed, white lamps, white satin pillows, perfect!

A beat

Best were those white bathrooms! Marble sink, marble tub, shower in the corner, the water coming out from six directions. And the shower door! Swans or something etched on it, so you couldn't see through. Opaque, I think it's called. Or translucent, I never remember which. Those swans hid you from here to here when you showered–

SHE *gestures bust line to hipline.*

– so no male intruders could peek from hiding places!

A beat

But the thing is...the important thing is...those bathrooms I saw on Saturday afternoons? The thing is...you promised you wouldn't laugh, okay?

SHE *leans in closer, going into an almost whisper as she nears her Truth.*

There was no...no toilet. None. Ever. You never saw one! I thought... well, this is what I thought: "Stars don't have to *go*. They never have to" – you know – "*make* anything." Not #1. Not #2. Jean Harlow? Nothing. Myrna Loy? Nothing. Joan Crawford? Nothing. Because they were *stars*. You said you wouldn't laugh.

A beat

I started to tell my first husband – why can't I remember his name? "When I'm in the movies, *I'll* be like that, too." "Like what?" he said. Oh, I *was* going to tell him, I *was*, that I wouldn't have to go to the toilet ever again either! But I saw this puzzled look and I couldn't tell him. I just smiled, like it was a joke, me being ignorant again. "Nothing," I said. And that was it. I never told anyone. Until just now. You said you wouldn't laugh.

A beat

But you know something? It wasn't a joke. I meant it. I *did*. One of those dumb reporters asked me once, "Do you want something special from your career?" And I said, "I just want to be wonderful." It was in all the papers the next day, quotation marks and everything. But no one guessed! No one ever guessed I meant that...that I would never have to make, you know, those #1's and #2's again. You're not laughing, are you? I hope not. You said you wouldn't.

A beat

So, then, when it was all happening, everything exploding like that, cameras and premieres and my name on the sidewalk – well, I couldn't tell *then*, could I? I wouldn't dare!

A beat. Her thoughts go far afield.

I don't see what's so bad about wanting never to have to make. I was beautiful, I don't mind saying it, everything about me was beautiful, everybody said so. I didn't want to – spoil it, that's all. Not up there on the screen, in the white bedrooms with the satin pillows, not down here, either, with my *own* white bedroom and my *own* satin pillows. But I *was* spoiling it, you see? Just the same as before, spoiling it with the #1 and the #2, and the noises and the smells, and the stains. I *hate* stains! Stains spoil things so much! Who wants that?

SHE *leans in closer.*

I spoiled it for every man in the whole entire world, dreaming about what I had under my dress, dreaming I had something special, something different, something *wonderful*, and…and…

SHE *goes silent for a long time.* SHE *puts her head down.*

You see? I spoiled it. For you *and* for me. That's my secret. That's what I needed to explain.

SHE *looks up.*

Aren't you supposed to feel better if you tell? I don't feel better. No. I don't.

A beat

This feeling of not living much longer? I don't mind. Really. So, if I lived 10 more years, 20, 30. So what? I'd still be the same as before. You see?

A beat. Now SHE *sees what has happened to her tape recorder: the reel unruly, useless coils, etc.*

Oh, no!

SHE *picks up the reel.*

Look at this! Will you look at this? I told that pricky gofer, I *told* him, I – Why are people like that?

SHE *puts the reel down on the bed. A sudden, childish impulse seizes her:* SHE *tosses the coils of tape over her head, like confetti.*

Whee!

SHE *stops as abruptly as she began.*

So much for "Miss Monroe Explains," right?

A beat

I think maybe I'll rest now.

But SHE *doesn't move.*

Can you still hear me?

SHE *picks up the microphone.*

Can you? Maybe not.

Now SHE *doesn't know quite what to do with herself.*

Yes. I will rest.

SHE *takes a pill from the vial at her bedside.*

I was saving this for later, but – why not?

SHE *swallows it without water.*

I don't need anything to wash them down with anymore, did you notice?

About to lie down, SHE *suddenly catches herself.*

Whoops! I better not wrinkle this dress! That cunt of a studio – I mean, that *august* studio – will send some pricky gofer to arrest me!

SHE *unbuttons the dress.*

Can you hear me? I don't have anything special or wonderful under here, you got that?

The dress slips to the floor. SHE *stands in the nude.*

And I *am* sorry I spoiled it all for you. That was all Miss Monroe wanted to explain.

SHE *puts the microphone down.* SHE *goes to the bed and lies down, pulling a sheet over her. The spotlight narrows until it takes in only her face.* SHE *waits for sleep, but it won't come.*

THE CURTAIN FALLS
END OF PLAY

THE BAND TAKES A SHORT BREAK

a one-act play

The Band Takes A Short Break

production history:

In February 2000, this play won First Prize in the Great Neck Public Access TV competition, and went on to take First Prize in the Northeast Regional Public Access competition. Since then, it has been shown repeatedly on Long Island and area public access TV channels. It was directed by Norman Hall with the following cast:

Carrie . . . . Tara Flynn
George . . . . .Charles F. Wagner IV

In February 2001, this play was presented jointly by Stageplays Theatre Company and the Episcopal Actors' Guild at Guild Hall, New York City. It was directed by Tom Ferriter with the following cast:

Carrie . . . . Sally Connors
George . . . . Lino Alvarez

setting:
A corner table at a local hotel bar.

time:
The present, early evening.

characters:
CARRIE, about 40
GEORGE, about 40

AT RISE: CARRIE *and* GEORGE *dance to the soothing music. In a state of sublime relaxation,* CARRIE *hums to herself.*

Then the music stops.

CARRIE: Oh, they always stop just when it's getting good. Why is that?

GEORGE: They need their break, that's all.

CARRIE: I won't stop dancing.

GEORGE: Come, Carrie, it's time to sit down.

CARRIE: I want never to sit down. What do you think of that?

GEORGE: I have to talk to you. For just a little while, okay?

CARRIE: I want never to talk. What do you think of that? I will stand here forever.

SHE *clings to him.*

GEORGE: Everybody's looking at us.

CARRIE: They're jealous, that's why!

Turning to the crowd.

You're all jealous of me!

Nobody hears this, of course. GEORGE *is firm now, leading* CARRIE *to the table.*

SHE *touches his forehead*

You are frowning.

GEORGE: Am I?

CARRIE: I don't like you nearly so much when you frown. You look ominous!

SHE *laughs.*

What do you think of that word?

GEORGE: What should I think?

CARRIE: You should think how clever I am, to learn a new word every week, so Jack will think I'm still going to night school.

GEORGE: Listen, Carrie–

CARRIE: You didn't know I was clever, did you!

GEORGE: Of course, I knew.

CARRIE: You're frowning again! When you look like that I think something's wrong.

SHE *puts her hand over his mouth.*

Nothing can be wrong. Nothing. So no talk yet, George. Promise?

GEORGE: *(Indulgently)* Finish your dessert. It's getting late.

CARRIE: You know what my doctor would say if he saw me eating like this, don't you? Self-defeating, Carrie, self-defeating.

About to eat.

Promise me you won't look serious again. I couldn't take it tonight.

GEORGE: I promise.

CARRIE: Tell me you like this place.

GEORGE: I do like it.

CARRIE: Because, do you have any idea how hard it is to find these out-of-the-way places, with a band that plays real music? Almost impossible!

GEORGE: I imagine that's true, yes.

CARRIE: You do know why it had to be especially nice tonight?

GEORGE: Don't say it's an anniversary, please. It isn't.

CARRIE: Why not? Why should anniversaries be wasted on married people?

SHE *looks around.*

They're jealous, all of them!

SHE *laughs.*

Weren't we lucky Jack is out-of-town again!

GEORGE: *(Hesitantly)* The thing is, Carrie–

CARRIE: The thing is, now you look glum! I am not going to bawl you out for forgetting our anniversary, if that's what you think. I don't expect you to remember.

A beat

Do you?

GEORGE: Of course, I do.

CARRIE: What do you remember? What?

GEORGE: That whenever I came to do the books for Safeway's–

CARRIE: There was this big smile! Whose?

GEORGE: You were always the nicest one at the checkout counter.

CARRIE: I wasn't fat then.

GEORGE: You were never fat, Carrie.

CARRIE: Then why did it take you forever to even talk to me?

GEORGE: I'm shy. You know that.

CARRIE: Well, it's a good thing I'm not! That was two years ago, two years and four days ago. See how I remember things? Tell the truth: you thought I wasn't married. Or maybe you knew I was, you dirty old man!

GEORGE: Please, Carrie. Not tonight.

CARRIE: Why not? When a dream comes true, a person should remember everything about it. I saw you first, you know. That's when I took off my wedding ring.

GEORGE *would protest the foolishness of all this, but* CARRIE *will not be dissuaded.*

"What do I have to do to get that man to ask me out?" I said to my packer. "You wouldn't dare go," she said. "Watch me," I said. Then I had to wait 100 years for you to do it! Are you glad I said "Yes?"

GEORGE: Yes.

CARRIE: *(Grasping his hand)* I bet you don't know the first thing, the very first thing I noticed about you. Guess.

GEORGE: I can't guess.

CARRIE: Oh, come on, guess!

GEORGE: My bald spot.

CARRIE: You do not have a bald spot. It was your eyebrows!

GEORGE: Nobody notices eyebrows.

CARRIE: I do. All the time. There's something about a man's eyebrows, not every man's eyebrows, that makes me wobble inside. Not Jack's, not any more. Yours!

CARRIE *musses up his eyebrows, but* GEORGE *smoothes them again.*

Even when I was young, I used to say, "Someday, I'll find the most perfect eyebrows in the world, and the man who owns them, that's the man I want and will have." What I meant was "marry" then. I thought "marry" meant you would mean something to somebody.

GEORGE: It does mean that.

CARRIE: *(Sarcastically)* Oh, yes, it does. Oh, yes! Why don't things work out the way they should, George?

GEORGE: They just don't sometimes. We have to be realistic.

CARRIE: I know, but why? I wish I was pretty.

GEORGE: You are pretty. You are.

CARRIE: I always meant to go to school, to learn things, to do things in a smarter way. I always knew there was better than working at a checkout counter. Why didn't I do something about it, when I was young, when there was time? I didn't think. Jack came along and I didn't think.

A beat

Jack has lady friends on the road, you know. It's not the way things ought to be, is it?

GEORGE: *(Trying to tell her something)* People don't always get what they deserve, Carrie. Sometimes, even when you don't want to hurt a person, a good person, you have to, because you just have to, that's all.

CARRIE: *(Laughing)* Who's talking about hurting a person? I'm not. I'm talking about waiting for something to happen, praying for something to happen, so you wind up taking anything that comes along!

Very quickly, to head off the possibility that SHE *has hurt* GEORGE. SHE *hasn't.*

I'm sorry. I didn't mean that, not for you, not about you. You're the one thing I do look forward to. You're it. It!

Laughing again.

I'm tired of all this jabber-jabber! I told you I didn't want it. Your eyebrows still make me wobble, George. Right now, inside it's wobble, wobble!

SHE *kisses her finger and plants it on his eyebrow.*

GEORGE: The thing is, Carrie, the thing I wanted to talk to you about is – this is our last night together.

CARRIE: Oh, George, not that "last-night-together" speech! Not again.

GEORGE: I mean it this time. I do.

CARRIE: You always mean it! I can make a chart: every two months, no, less, every six weeks, it's the "last-night-together" speech.

SHE *covers her ears.*

Tonight, I will not listen to it!

GEORGE: I'm going to get married, Carrie.

CARRIE: I can't hear a word. Not a word.

Keeping her ears covered.

I'm the one who ought to make the "last-night-together" speeches. A married woman? With children? Willing to do whatever you like, go wherever you like? Instead, one little corner of me wants to stand up and say, "Look, everybody: fat Carrie has a lover! A lover!" Don't worry, George, I wouldn't do that to you!

GEORGE: *(Removing her hands from her ears)* I've met someone, Carrie. I'm going to get married.

CARRIE: *(After a long beat)* You're – ? What?

GEORGE: You heard, Carrie.

CARRIE: No!

GEORGE: I've met someone. I've been seeing her and we're going to get married.

CARRIE: *(With shocked laughter)* I don't know what to say!

GEORGE: *(Getting it all out now)* She's an account executive. She works for one of my other clients. I saw her–

CARRIE: Like me. You saw her like you saw me.

GEORGE: One particular Saturday morning, four months ago, I was doing their books. She was on the telephone to–

CARRIE: Account executive. I bet you think I don't know what that means.

GEORGE: I don't think that.

CARRIE: Account executive. That's something, isn't it! She's smart, isn't she!

GEORGE: She's very smart, yes.

CARRIE: She is not like the dumbo at the checkout counter!

GEORGE: Don't, Carrie!

CARRIE: Not like some slob sneaking off while her husband is out-of-town!

GEORGE: You mustn't say things like that!

CARRIE: Why not? They're true, aren't they?

GEORGE: I never meant to hurt you, Carrie.

CARRIE: *(Not listening)* Four months ago, you say.

GEORGE: Yes.

CARRIE: What's the matter then, George? She won't let you touch her yet?

GEORGE: *(Quietly, firmly)* Don't do this.

CARRIE: Or did you want to have Carrie the slob at the same time, so you'd have something to tell your friends?

GEORGE: Please don't do this.

CARRIE: Last May, when Jack was away and I was at your flat every night? You knew her then?

GEORGE: Carrie, I–

CARRIE: DID YOU KNOW HER THEN!

GEORGE: Yes. I knew her then.

CARRIE: And you let me come anyway!

GEORGE: I didn't want you to come. I didn't ask you to come.

CARRIE: No, you didn't ask me. Funny – I didn't realize that before.

GEORGE: I tried to tell you. I couldn't find a way.

CARRIE: You couldn't find a way! Why not? With all that education, with all those big words you know? Not one little sentence to tell the slob to stay home!

GEORGE: I don't think I want to listen any more.

CARRIE: You're only a bookkeeper who's losing his hair, you know!

GEORGE: (Standing up) It's time to go. Now.

CARRIE: (Quickly) Oh, no, George. No. No. Sit down. Please!

GEORGE: We'll only make each other more unhappy.

CARRIE: No, we won't. We won't! It's the shock, that's all. It'll be all right in a minute. Really. I promise.

GEORGE is being cajoled into sitting down again.

A beat

What's her name?

GEORGE: Lynne.

CARRIE: "Lynne." I've always hated "Carrie", you know. I tell everyone, "Call me 'Carolyn', please," but they never do. Even you won't.

GEORGE: I never remember.

CARRIE: (A beat) Is Lynne pretty?

GEORGE: Yes and no. Average, maybe.

CARRIE: Well, that isn't right, is it? You deserve a very pretty woman at your side.

GEORGE: I don't deserve anything.

CARRIE: You do. I say you do.

GEORGE: I'm ordinary, Carrie, I know I am.

CARRIE: *(Not listening, off on her own again)* You should not settle for less-than-very-pretty, George. I know. When you're not smart and you get fat just looking at food, you know!

SHE *takes a roll from the table and throws it to the floor.*

GEORGE: Carrie!

CARRIE: The thing is, you see, I have gone back to night school, George. You didn't know that, did you! And I have started a new diet. You didn't know that, either!

SHE *buries her face in her hands.*

GEORGE: *(A beat)* I want a home, Carrie. I'm almost 40. I want a home.

CARRIE: A home! That's what you know about it. You'll turn around and you'll be old and bored, and your precious Lynne will be looking for an out-of-the-way place with a band!

GEORGE: Stop! Please! I want you to stop.

CARRIE: I'm nothing by myself, George, nothing! I can't live by myself. I can't live with myself!

GEORGE: You should talk to someone about these feelings, Carrie.

CARRIE: Who?

GEORGE: Jack, maybe.

CARRIE: Jack! *(Laughing)* Talk to Jack about my feelings? Why in the world would I do that?

GEORGE: Your doctor, then.

CARRIE: My doctor! Once, I said to him, "I'm not starved for food, doctor. I'm starved for miracles!" You know what he said? "We're all starved for miracles!"

GEORGE: I think you–

CARRIE: You haven't listened, George. I am going to go back to night school. And I am going to go on a new diet, that's the truth. So you see? I can deserve you!

GEORGE: *(Cupping her face in his hands)* I'm the one who doesn't deserve you.

Carrie would protest.

I want to get married, Carrie. It's time I got married.

CARRIE: *(Studying his face,* SHE *comes to a moment of reasonability)* Of course, you want to get married.

GEORGE: Don't cry.

CARRIE: Have I ever asked for anything?

GEORGE: No.

CARRIE: Have I ever made a demand of you, one single demand?

GEORGE: No.

CARRIE: I'm going to ask you for something now, George. I have a right to ask!

GEORGE: Of course you do.

CARRIE: Marry this Lynne if you want to. I won't care. It won't matter. We'll make it not matter.

GEORGE: It will matter.

CARRIE: It won't matter. Just don't say I won't see you again. Just don't say that.

GEORGE: I have to say it, Carrie.

CARRIE: We can find a way, you see? You won't have to worry. I'll take care of things the way I always do.

GEORGE: No, Carrie! No!

HE *looks at his watch.*

I have to go. We're driving upstate in the morning to see her family.

CARRIE: We can't leave yet.

GEORGE: We have to!

CARRIE: But listen! The band is coming back. They're starting again. One more dance. Just one more dance. Please?

GEORGE *stands stoically.*

My one and only demand on you, George. Please?

GEORGE *gives in to her pleading.* THEY *dance.* CARRIE *searches his face for signs, any signs, that he might bend from his resolve. There are no such signs.*

GEORGE *dances with her now in order not to hurt her badly. Someday, somewhere, someone will.*

I wish the band would never stop.

GEORGE: They always do.

CARRIE: *(A beat, as* THEY *dance)* George?

Looking him full in the face.

I'll have to start noticing again, won't I?

GEORGE: Noticing what?

CARRIE: Wobble, wobble!

GEORGE: What?

CARRIE: *(Almost expressionless now,* SHE *looks over his shoulder)* Eyebrows. I'll never find eyebrows like yours again in the whole world.

A beat

But then, you have to be realistic, isn't that what you said, George?

SHE *buries herself in his shoulder in momentary retreat as* THEY *dance.*

THE CURTAIN FALLS
END OF PLAY

TWO SISTERS SITTING ON A BENCH, RESTING FROM ALL THE EXCITEMENT

a one-act play

Two Sisters Sitting On A Bench, Resting From All The Excitement

production history:

In December 2003, this play was presented by Stageplays Theatre Company at The Lambs in New York City. It was directed by Tom Ferriter with the following cast:

Marjorie .... Beth Holland
Rose .... Joyce Randolph

setting:

A bench beneath a tree on The Common, where the Crafts Fair is in progress.

time:

A nice summer day, late morning.

characters:

ROSE
about 70, stolid, heavy-set

MARJORIE
about 65, petite, playful

AT RISE: ROSE *is seated on the bench, her big pink hat on her lap. Next to her on the bench is an identical hat,* MARJORIE'S, *"reserving" her seat.*

An excited MARJORIE *enters, carrying a cardboard box.*

MARJORIE: Rose! I got them! I got them!

ROSE: Calmness, Marjorie, calmness.

MARJORIE: They're the same size as my Bavarian fruit plates at home! *Exactly* the same size!

ROSE: I don't see how that can be.

MARJORIE: *(Putting her hat on the ground and sitting)* But they are! I *know* they are! I can't tell you how excited I am!

ROSE: Calmness, Marjorie, calmness.

MARJORIE: *(Handing* ROSE *dollar bills)* Here's your change. I did *exactly* what you said. He was asking $25, but I haggled him down.

Pulling a plate from the box.

See? The same!

ROSE: Well, it isn't.

MARJORIE: It is! It *is!*

ROSE: Not to dash cold water on your excitement, Marjorie, the Bavarian fruit plates at home are larger, a good deal larger.

MARJORIE: How do you know? How do you *know* that?

ROSE: Haven't I seen them in the china cabinet every day? Wasn't I the one who bought them for you?

MARJORIE: You did?

ROSE: I did. At the Crafts Fair two years ago.

MARJORIE: I don't remember that.

ROSE: I do.

MARJORIE: *(Disappointed)* Should I take them back, then?

ROSE: At a Crafts Fair you don't take things back, Marjorie. You accept what you've purchased.

MARJORIE: I suppose.

ROSE: If you thought you might find matching Bavarian fruit plates today, it was up to you to bring one of them with you, so that you could match it. Then you wouldn't have all this fuss. Put your head down, Marjorie.

MARJORIE: What?

ROSE: *(Putting her head down)* Just do it. Keep it down till I tell you.

MARJORIE: But the men are starting their ring toss game. I wanted to go.

ROSE: Wait till that dreadful Vivian something-or-other passes. I don't want to have to take notice of her.

MARJORIE: *(Putting her head down)* She's not as bad as all that, is she?

ROSE: You're not the one who has to deal with her over and over about spots on our blouses after we've paid a fortune to have them dry-cleaned.

MARJORIE: It's because her eyes are going.

ROSE: If her eyes are going, she has no business running a dry-cleaning store.

MARJORIE: I suppose.

ROSE: To say nothing about having to hear her say over and over again, "My daughter will be back from college next year!" As if we'd be at all interested!

MARJORIE: I was certain the plates were exactly the same size.

A beat

No! You are wrong!

ROSE: What?

MARJORIE: You didn't buy the plates for me at the Crafts Fair two years ago. You bought me that beautiful paisley scarf!

ROSE: I bought that scarf last year.

MARJORIE: You did?

ROSE: I did.

MARJORIE: Oh.

A beat

Is she gone?

ROSE: *(Looking up again)* Yes, thank God.

MARJORIE: Now my neck is hurting.

ROSE: Rest a minute.

A beat

Which paisley scarf, I might add, I've never seen you wear.

MARJORIE: I am waiting for a special occasion, because I love it so. It's sitting in tissue paper on the shelf next to my hatbox.

ROSE: You're sure you haven't lost it?

MARJORIE: Of course, I haven't lost it.

ROSE: I don't believe you don't wear it because you love it. I believe you don't wear it because you hate it.

MARJORIE: *(Caught! A guilty beat)* I should have brought one of my Bavarian fruit plates with me. You're right.

ROSE: Your face is all sweaty, you know.

MARJORIE: I think I'll watch the ring toss now.

ROSE: Wait till I wipe your cheeks. They're getting puffy.

Wiping MARJORIE'S *face.*

I'm saying that the Bavarian plates don't match as well as you think they do. I'm not saying you couldn't line up the plates on different shelves. They might go together very well.

MARJORIE: *(Grabbing the handkerchief)* I'll wipe my own face, if you don't mind!

SHE *wipes her face. Then* SHE *stands, ready to go, a bit more angry than she should be.*

I ought to know when you bought that paisley scarf, Rose. And I say you bought it two years ago!

SHE *reaches to the ground and puts her pink hat on the bench.* SHE *exits.*

THE LIGHTS FADE SLOWLY

When they come up again, ROSE *is on the bench alone.*

ROSE: *(Looking into space)* "Oh, Rose is the difficult one, Rose is just so stubborn!" That's what everybody thinks. I can see it in their faces. "Rose is the heavy one, the bossy one, so she makes all the decisions." Do they ever ask why? Sure, Rose makes all the decisions: somebody has to!

Calling out.

Not that way, Marjorie! The hill is too steep!

A beat. Then, more gently.

If I let her, she would ramble off and never find her way back. How many times has she locked herself out of the house without her key?

How many times has she lost her key? Her purse? I don't want to think what would happen if I didn't hold onto her cash, and dole it out to her!

A beat

If I let her, she would spend all her money! Those plates! She didn't haggle anyone down to $15 – she paid the full $25 asked, and used the bills she hides away from me to pay the difference! I know her ways!

A beat

"Why is Rose so bossy?" Why? I'd like to tell them why some day. She can't get a meat platter down from the top shelf without breaking it, that's why! She can't even drive a car, won't even learn to, that's why!

A beat

Oh yes, Rose is the strong one! Just once, just once, Rose would like to be the weak one, the one with the tiny smile and the little girl's voice! I'd show her. "Waiting for the special occasion" to wear the paisley scarf. Hah! Does she think I don't know what happened to that scarf? Does she really think I don't know what she did with it?

Calling out.

"I know what you did with that paisley scarf, Marjorie, don't think I do not!"

A beat

Some morning, the strong one is going to get up and go. Leave. Go. Just take off where the road leads me. Then we'll see. We'll see how she gets along without the bossy one to care for her. Then we'll all see!

THE LIGHTS FADE SLOWLY

When they come up again, both pink hats are on the bench.

ROSE *and* MARJORIE *enter, carrying plates of food.* THEY *put the hats on the ground and sit down.*

ROSE: You see what a good idea it was to bring these big old hats?

MARJORIE: I have to admit it, Rose: a very good idea.

ROSE: Reserved seats, waiting at all times!

MARJORIE: Reserved seats, waiting at all times!

ROSE: And if some dishonest person should take them, what's the loss?

MARJORIE: What's the loss?

ROSE: They're the oldest hats we own.

THEY *sit quietly and eat from their plates.*

MARJORIE: *(A beat)* Actually, this is not the oldest hat I own.

ROSE: *(Handing* MARJORIE *a napkin)* It isn't?

MARJORIE: This is the hat I wore the day I came back home to live with you.

ROSE: Is it?

MARJORIE: I brought this one for you, to thank you for having me.

ROSE: Of course. I remember.

MARJORIE: The oldest hat I own, which, of course, I could never leave on a bench at a Crafts Fair, is the hat I wore to my poor Henry's funeral.

SHE *crosses herself.*

ROSE: There's a bit of food on your chin.

SHE *wipes* MARJORIE'S *chin.*

MARJORIE: That hat is safely in a hatbox on the shelf in my closet, where it will always be. In blue tissue paper.

ROSE: Your chicken will get cold, Marjorie.

MARJORIE: Poor Henry. Fourteen years, and I still miss him, do you know that? Oh, don't misunderstand: it was sweet of you, very sweet – very dear and very sweet – to invite me back in the house when my poor Henry crossed over, and I do enjoy living with you, truly I do. But sometimes – well, Rose, sometimes, I miss him.

ROSE: A sister is not a husband, but I do try.

MARJORIE: Yes, you do! And you succeed, too!

ROSE: *(Taking a bite of chicken and becoming excited)* Well, for heaven's sakes!

MARJORIE: What?

ROSE: The obstinate Frank something-or-other has finally listened to me!

MARJORIE: Has he?

ROSE: There is mustard in this marinade!

MARJORIE: Is there? I don't taste it.

ROSE: *(Taking another bite)* Well, I do. Yes, I do! For as long as that obstinate man has been cooking for the Crafts Fairs, that's as long as I told him my recipe for marinade, and that's as long as he has ignored it. Now he has actually done it – there is mustard in this marinade!

MARJORIE: *(Standing up and pretending to call out)* "Listen, everybody: Frank something-or-other has at last recognized Rose's recipe for marinade!"

ROSE: Marjorie, sit down!

MARJORIE: "This is her secret recipe, which even I, as her loyal younger sister, do not share!"

ROSE: Marjorie, if you don't sit down, I'll take my hat and move!

MARJORIE: *(Laughingly)* No, no! I'm sitting down. See?

SHE *sits.*

ROSE: *(A beat)* I'm not asking for credit. I don't need credit. If you think I want credit, you're wrong.

MARJORIE: And what if he has more sales this year than he's ever had before? Then credit is due!

ROSE: Not that I would mind if he came over and said, "You were right, Rose. After all these years, I see you are right." That isn't going to happen. It's my experience that men never give credit.

THEY *eat quietly for a moment.*

MARJORIE: *(A beat. Glum, again)* My poor Henry would have.

ROSE: Would have what?

MARJORIE: Given credit.

ROSE: Then, he was unique.

MARJORIE: Yes. He was.

SHE *stares off to the side.*

ROSE: What are you staring at?

MARJORIE: Nothing.

ROSE: It can't be nothing. That's a very intent stare.

MARJORIE: It's the men at the ring toss.

ROSE: What about them?

MARJORIE: Do you see how they hang over the rail? They don't seem to care how they look in the back.

ROSE: How do you mean?

MARJORIE: They don't care about the seams of their pants, and what happens to those seams.

ROSE: What about the seams?

MARJORIE: Didn't you ever notice that when men lean over like that – not all men, just some men – the seam of their pants enters – no, "intrudes" is the better word – into the, you know, the crack of their behinds.

ROSE: Marjorie! For heaven sakes!

MARJORIE: Watch. When they stand up to get another hoop? See what happens?

ROSE: Of all the idiotic things I've ever heard!

MARJORIE: Well, it's true.

ROSE: *(Dropping her fork)* Now look what you made me do.

MARJORIE: Take mine.

ROSE: I'll get another one on my own, thank you.

> SHE *stands, puts her hat on the bench, and begins to exit.*

"Intruding seams!" You make me glad I never married.

> SHE *exits.*

THE LIGHTS FADE SLOWLY

When they come up again, MARJORIE *sits on the bench alone.*

MARJORIE: *(Looking into space)* "You make me glad I never married." I don't believe that for a moment, Rose! When did you even have an opportunity to refuse? When did a man even ask you to a dance, much less offer to marry you!

A beat

And I don't believe for a moment that you never noticed how the seam of men's pants intrudes into the crack of their behinds, either. You only pretend not to notice! You won't go straight to hell if you do look for these things. Okay, Rose?

A beat

Well – what do you expect from a person who copies a recipe off a mustard jar and passes it off as her own! Oh, yes, Rose, I know about that. Did you think I was napping? I watched you copy that recipe word for word!

A beat

I'll tell you this: no seam ever intruded into my Henry's behind. I was there to watch over things like that. I took pride, Rose, in that nice flat behind of his, what do you think of that? I took pride, vast pride, in making sure his pants had a proper fit, so no seam would dare intrude, what do you think of that? Don't you scoff at me, sister dear. Taking care of a husband beats copying recipes off mustard jars and nagging that poor volunteer something-or-other year after year to cook chicken breasts your way. Not everything has to be your way, only your way.

Eating a piece of chicken.

On top of which, this marinade doesn't taste all that good, if you ask me.

A beat

You know what your trouble is? You have nothing to do, nothing to interest you, nothing – no life! Everybody thinks so, just everybody! They would say so, to your face, if they dared to! But they are scared of you, Rose! You are scary – scary and stubborn and demanding. And bossy! So there!

A beat. SHE *takes a plate out of the box.*

They are the same size, I don't care what you say. And I didn't pay $15 for them – I paid the full $25. So what? Who wants to haggle all the way through life? I don't! I had $10 tucked away in the tissue paper in my hatbox, so what do you think about that?

Standing up and calling out.

"I paid $25 for my new Bavarian fruit plates, Rose. Like it or lump it, sister dear!"

SHE *sits. A beat.*

Was it really only last year that she bought that awful paisley scarf? It seems longer. I hate that scarf. Do you hear me, Rose? I hate it! And I'm not waiting for some special occasion to wear it. I am never going to wear it. I got rid of it, didn't I? I think I did – think I remember throwing it out months ago. Or did I? Well, if I didn't, I'm going to toss it away the minute I get home, what do you think about that, Rose?

A beat

They're having such fun at the ring toss, those men. I'd go back over there and talk to them, but guess who wouldn't like it?

Suddenly laughing.

That man on the end, in the Bermuda shorts, Rose! Look how far that seam is intruding! It is intruding where the sun doesn't shine! If I had the courage, Rose, I would tell you this: it would do you good to stare at something like that for a while!

SHE *sighs deeply.*

THE LIGHTS FADE SLOWLY

When they come up again, MARJORIE *and* ROSE *are sitting on the bench, their pink hats atop their heads.* ROSE *holds a small painting on her lap.*

ROSE: I think I've been foolish.

MARJORIE: You haven't, Rose, it's a very nice painting.

ROSE: I think I've been foolish.

MARJORIE: Oh, stop! You're only saying that so I'll contradict you.

ROSE: Where would we even hang it?

MARJORIE: Lots of places! In the front hall. In the bathroom.

ROSE: You don't hang a painting in the bathroom.

MARJORIE: Sure, you do. I see it in pictures all the time. In magazines.

ROSE: Magazines aren't real life, Marjorie. Who can I depend on to stop me from being foolish if not you?

MARJORIE: How could I stop you? I wasn't there.

ROSE: You saw me talking to that so-called art dealer. You must have seen me.

MARJORIE: Plus, if I had been there, I wouldn't have stopped you. It's not foolish – it's fun.

ROSE: *(A beat.* SHE *studies the painting)* $47 and I'm not even sure I like it.

MARJORIE: The frame alone is worth more than $47.

ROSE: Do you think so?

MARJORIE: I do think so.

ROSE: *(A beat)* Sometimes, I think we ought to stop coming to Crafts Fairs altogether. It's just a bunch of people getting rid of things they don't want to a bunch of other people who won't want them after a week.

MARJORIE: I'll tell you what, Rose: if you don't care to put the painting in the hall or in the bathroom, I'll buy it from you. I'll give it to my nephew for Christmas.

ROSE: You don't mean Mitchell.

MARJORIE: Yes. Mitchell.

ROSE: Mitchell won't like it.

MARJORIE: How can you know that?

ROSE: There are things I just know.

MARJORIE: He's my nephew, Rose. He's my Henry's brother's son.

ROSE: You don't have to define a nephew for me, Marjorie. I know what a nephew is.

Looking at the painting.

You can give him the painting. I'll keep the frame.

MARJORIE: That makes no sense. The frame is part of the charm of the picture.

ROSE: The picture doesn't have charm, Marjorie. It has – a bit of importance, I hope.

MARJORIE: I think it has charm.

ROSE: Yes. A bit of importance.

A beat

I guess I will keep it. The whole thing. End of discussion.

MARJORIE: You're in a mood today!

ROSE: I am not in a mood.

MARJORIE: I know when you're in a mood and when you're not in a mood. Today, you're in a mood.

ROSE: If I am, which I'm not, it's because I haven't wanted to think of you giving a present to a nephew like Mitchell.

MARJORIE: I have the right to give him a present anytime I want.

ROSE: Has he so much as called you to thank you for the present you sent him last Christmas?

MARJORIE: Whether he thanks me or not is my concern, Rose, not yours. He is, after all, my only living relative.

ROSE: Oh?

MARJORIE: *(Quickly, embarrassed by what she has said)* I mean, outside of you.

THE LIGHTS FADE SLOWLY

When they come up again, they come up on ROSE. MARJORIE *sits at her side, not moving a hair.*

ROSE: *(Looking at* MARJORIE*)* No, I'm not crying. What makes you think I'm crying? It was a slip of the tongue, this "only living relative" business. I know that. I'll be all right. I will be all right.

Looking into space.

Oh, if I could only ask you a question, Marjorie! I would love to ask you, but why bother? You wouldn't have any notion of what I was talking about! But if I could ask. Marjorie: Be honest, now! Be truthful! Have you ever thought to yourself, "I lead an unimportant life." Have you? "I go to the Crafts Fair once a year, and I buy something and I go home and watch television and go to bed and – that's it! There's all that other time, that time when there is – there is – nothing. Nothing going on but the weather. All I do is take up space." Do you ever say that to yourself, Marjorie? "Most of the time, all I do is take up space?" No, you don't – you're not the type of person to look inside yourself. I look inside, all the time. That's why I'm crying. You don't have any notion of what I'm talking about, do you? Of course not. You don't have to look inside. You're likeable. People like you. They don't like me. I see that every day, Marjorie, in all their faces. "Marjorie is the likeable sister," those faces tell me. It's true. And what it means is: you don't ever have to think about the things I think about. What it means is: you don't have to cry like me, all of a sudden, for no good reason.

A beat

All I have done is take up space. All I will do is take up space. I won't ever do anything important. The difference is, Marjorie, I know it. You can just go ahead and have whatever vulgar thoughts you like, the seams in men's pants, intruding, whatever that's supposed to mean. Is that something a grown person should be thinking about? No! But it doesn't make you cry, Marjorie. Why not? It's unimportant, don't you see that? It's unimportant! You're only taking up space, too. So why don't you cry?

A beat

I've let all this happen! Without me to lean on, you would have some thought of your own about the life you lead, about–

Getting angry.

For God's sakes, Marjorie! I do all the driving, to church, to the stores, to everything! I take you to the supermarket and the dry cleaners, to this God-forsaken Crafts Fair! Do any of those people out there know what a burden you are to me? Do you know?

A beat

That beautiful paisley scarf! You don't even suspect that I pulled it out of the garbage can months ago, months ago, Marjorie. Don't ask me what I'll do with it. Maybe I'll put it back in the tissue paper on the shelf next to your hatbox. That'll give you a shock!

She laughs.

No! Someday, I'll just put it around my own neck and parade around in it. At the Crafts Fair! That'll give you a bigger shock!

A long beat as SHE *gets serious again.*

Sometimes, I find myself wishing you would…you know…just – die. I wouldn't be so burdened then! I wouldn't have to watch out for you every minute, wondering if you were wasting your money, or losing it, misplacing your purse, your keys. I would make a life for myself. Unburdened, yes – I would be unburdened! That's what I want!

A beat

But then – if you did die? How would I manage if you weren't here anymore? How would I fill my day? There'd be nothing to do. There'd be nothing at all to do. Nothing.

A beat

Nothing.

THE LIGHTS FADE SLOWLY

When they come up again, they come up on MARJORIE.

ROSE *sits at her side, not moving a hair.*

MARJORIE: *(Looking at* ROSE*)* Oh, Rose, I have hurt your feelings so terribly! If I could cut my tongue out, I would. "Only living relative!" It was a dumb, dumb thing to say and not true!

Looking into space.

"Oh, Marjorie is the weak one, the stupid one, Marjorie is" – that's what everybody thinks. I can see it in their faces. "Yes, Marjorie, so small, so fragile, while Rose is so strong and so healthy." Marjorie can't make decisions, they think. Well, of course, Marjorie can't make decisions. *She* makes them, Rose makes them, all of them! That's the way she wants it, and that's the way she gets it! Can she ever understand an opposing point of view? Never!

A beat

She won't spend a dime without planning two months for it, three months! It's not natural. It's not normal. She bought that painting this morning for one reason and one reason only: she wanted that so-called art dealer to talk with her, to flirt with her. She likes his blue eyes. She thinks I don't know about that. Oh, I know! What she doesn't know is that those paintings go all over the state, week after week after week at Crafts Fairs, all summer long, where he glues those blue eyes on every woman, fat or thin, tall, short, and gets them to part with their cash. You hear me, Rose? He made a fuss over you so he could get your $47 – so much for your careful ways with money! Did you think he would touch your shoulder after you bought it? Embrace you? You don't have any idea what it's like to be embraced by a man who wants to embrace you. You've never been embraced by a man who wanted to embrace you, have you? Have you?

A beat

Always right, convinced that she alone is right!

Pretends to call out.

"You're not always right, Rose!"

A beat

"Marjorie spends money like water." I don't spend money like water. I spend the usual amounts that human beings spend. She's the one. She's the one who buys things at Church Fairs, and gives them to me, so she won't feel guilty! True or false? True! That awful paisley scarf! Ugh!

A beat

If she mentions that scarf one more time, I'll scream! What did I do with it? Did I throw it out? How would I get the courage to do that? Maybe it's up there in the tissue paper on my shelf. Oh, God, I don't remember!

A beat

"Marjorie never remembers to check the doors before we go to bed." What does she think will happen if the front door stays unlocked all night? Some man will come in at the stroke of midnight and fuck her? There, Rose! I have used a word you don't like, what do you think of that? Listen to me, Rose: if the front door is unlocked, no man is going to come in and fuck you. He'll fuck me!

SHE *laughs. Then, a beat.*

Sometimes, I find myself wishing she would…you would just – die. I wouldn't be so burdened then. I wouldn't have to listen to your criticism any more. I could breathe. I could live! I would make a life for myself. Unburdened, yes. I would be unburdened! That's what I want.

A beat

But then – if you did die? How would I manage, if you weren't here any more? How would I fill my day? There'd be nothing to do. There'd be nothing at all to do. Nothing.

A beat

Nothing.

THE LIGHTS FADE SLOWLY

When they come up again, ROSE *and* MARJORIE *are sitting quietly next to each other.*

EACH *of them having thought through her limited options apart from the other,* THEY *show a new spirit of rapprochement.* THEY *will, after all, face whatever tomorrows they have remaining to them together.*

ROSE: *(Looking at her watch)* It's almost 5 o'clock, Marjorie. Shall we have our ice cream cones?

MARJORIE: Just what I was going to say. What flavor do you think you might have, Rose?

ROSE: Chocolate, I think.

MARJORIE: Strawberry for me, I think. My treat.

ROSE: Very well. Your treat.

SHE *puts her purse back on the ground and looks to the side.*

Well, do you see that?

MARJORIE: What?

ROSE: That bunch of rude teenagers muscling into the ice cream line. This very minute! Just pushing ahead of all the others!

MARJORIE: Then shall we not wait for ice cream cones, Rose? I'm suddenly a bit tired.

ROSE: I feel winded myself.

MARJORIE: It's all the excitement.

ROSE: *(Wiping her face)* We'll just rest our legs a while longer, shall we?

A beat

I've been thinking, Marjorie. I guess you are right, after all.

MARJORIE: Right about what?

ROSE: The Bavarian fruit plates. I think they are the same size as the ones at home. We don't know, of course, until we get home, but I do believe they'll match nicely.

MARJORIE: Do you? Do you really?

ROSE: If they don't, I'll be much surprised.

MARJORIE: *(A beat)* You know something, Rose? I have heard people raving all day, just raving about the chicken breasts. It's your recipe they're raving about!

ROSE: Really? What people?

MARJORIE: Just people. One of them said, "Something is different, something is better."

ROSE: Well, good. It's the mustard, you know.

MARJORIE: Yes. I know.

ROSE: *(A beat)* If you like, you can give the whole picture to Mitchell.

MARJORIE: You mean, frame included?

ROSE: Frame included. My treat.

MARJORIE: Why, thank you, Rose.

A beat

This was a lovely Crafts Fair, wasn't it?

ROSE: Yes. It was.

MARJORIE: I can't wait to do it all again next summer. It's such a happy thing to plan for.

ROSE: Only next summer, we'll get our cones early, before crowds make it impossible.

MARJORIE: Good thinking! And we'll bring these two old hats with us again. They worked wonderfully well.

ROSE: They did, didn't they!

MARJORIE: And guess what? Next year I will wear my lovely paisley scarf. That's just what I will do!

ROSE: That will be very nice.

THE LIGHTS FADE SLOWLY

When they come up again on the bench, there is one pink hat. After a beat, MARJORIE *comes onto the scene, with an ice cream cone.* SHE *is wearing the paisley scarf.*

SHE *comes to the bench.* SHE *picks up the hat and puts it atop her head.* SHE *sits alone and eats.* SHE *looks blankly into space:* SHE *has absolutely nothing to do.*

THE LIGHTS FADE SLOWLY
END OF PLAY

LUNCHEON WITH MR. MOZART

a one-act play

Luncheon with Mr. Mozart

production history:

In May 2007, this play was presented by Around The Block Theatre Arts Workgroup at the New York Public Library (Seward Park Branch), New York City. It was directed by Mario Golden with the following cast:

Mr. Mozart . . . . Carlos Molina

Bryce. . . . . .Fausto Pineda

setting:
The place is Heaven, albeit a quirky Heaven.

A stereotypical Hollywood version will do nicely: a bit of smoky cloud hugging the floor; haloes (inexpensive ones) atop heads; white flowing robes and sandals for dress. A small bistro table and two chairs are the only furnishings.

time:
The present

sounds:

Every now and then, certain heavenly sounds are heard. Chimes ring on the monitors worn by residents, heralding an important celestial tally. (The final note played is, however, always gratingly off-key.)

At one point, a rendition of "Bei Mir Bist Du Schoen" is heard, sung by a trio of songstresses in slinky World War II gowns.

characters:
MR. MOZART
(not the one we expect, and pronounced Mo-*zart*), about 70.

BRYCE FITZWILLIAM
(about what we'd expect, given the name), a bit over 40.

and

The TRIO of SINGING SIRENS.

AT RISE: MOZART *sits at the table, coffee mug and musical score at hand.* BRYCE *approaches, carrying a lunch tray.* HE *watches and listens cautiously as chimes sound;* HE *winces at the dreadful last note.*

MOZART *examines the monitor around his neck, smiles contentedly, and kisses it before returning it to his robe.*

BRYCE: *(Nervously clearing his throat)* Sir?

MOZART: Yes?

BRYCE: You're expecting me.

MOZART: I am?

BRYCE: I'm Bryce Fitzwilliam. I'm your table partner for luncheon.

MOZART: Are you, now!

BRYCE: I see you've almost finished. I'm not *very* late, I hope.

Standing at the table.

This is an honor, sir, a *real* honor.

MOZART: Is it, now!

BRYCE: Unforgettable!

MOZART: Actually, it's *quite* forgettable. You see–

BRYCE: *(With a nervous laugh)* But that's so funny! Forgettable! *You,* whom the world reveres and celebrates!

MOZART: I seriously doubt that, because you see–

BRYCE: *I* especially have revered and celebrated you.

MOZART: It all sounds very nice, but–

BRYCE: Although I must say–

MOZART: Although you must say?

BRYCE: I must say that the picture you make isn't at all what it's supposed to be.

MOZART: The picture I make is *exactly* what it's supposed to be, because you see–

BRYCE: Oh, poring over that musical score is perfect, *perfect*! But the long hair, the *very* long hair: where is it? The curls, classic and classical curls: where are they?

MOZART: Classic and classical? On *this* head? There's a hot one!

BRYCE: Well, I *do* know these things. I've kept portraits of you on my piano since I was ten. And as Associate Professor of Musicology for lo! these–

MOZART *begins to laugh.*

The example of your artistry before my students every semester for lo! these–

MOZART'S *laughter builds.*

I *kept* that example before them! It inspired my *own* compositions, I hasten to add!

MOZART *is close to hysteria now.*

I'm not aware that I've said anything remotely funny, sir!

MOZART: *(Holding up a hand to try to contain himself)* Forgive me, please. This is your first day up here, isn't it?

BRYCE: Well, yes, it is, but–

MOZART: Let me guess. Shortly after your arrival, someone approached you. Howie, perhaps? I bet it was! He's big on musical stuff.

BRYCE: Well, yes. A man named Howie *did* approach me.

MOZART: Yes, Howie! It makes sense: he's overdue for his "scam option."

BRYCE: I beg your pardon?

MOZART: Let me guess. He asked you if you wanted to sit at Mr. Mozart's table for luncheon.

BRYCE: For *dinner*, too.

MOZART: *(Laughing again)* For dinner, too! The scoundrel!

BRYCE: Why is *that* funny?

MOZART: We don't *have* dinner here. Luncheon is *it* till tomorrow morning.

BRYCE: I don't understand. I–

Weakly

Isn't this Heaven?

MOZART: Oh, yes. This is Heaven.

BRYCE: No dinner? In *Heaven*?

MOZART: It keeps the belly fat down. Don't worry, though: breakfast is a lollapalooza! All-you-can-eat-buffet. You know, like in Vegas.

BRYCE: Like in Vegas?

MOZART: Get there early, friend. 8 o'clock sharp, you'll see them running like big-ass birds! Oh – sorry, Mr. Fitz–

BRYCE: You are *not* Mr. Mozart.

MOZART: Well, I am, and then again, I am not.

BRYCE: You are *not* Wolfgang Amadeus–

MOZART: Guilty as charged.

BRYCE: You are *far* from the Mozart I'm to lunch with!

MOZART: Again, guilty as charged. Mo-*zart* is my name, Moe Mo-*zart*, real name, Maurice. Notice, please, the pronunciation, Mo-*zart*, accent on the last syllable. No classical curls, no classical music. I was into R&B down there: my grandchildren hooked me on it, Mr. – listen, I can't keep calling you Mr. Fitzwilliam. Your friends call you "Fitz," am I right?

BRYCE: *(Coldly) Nobody* calls me "Fitz." Nobody has *ever* called me "Fitz."

MOZART: Hm! Interesting! Then I'll call you "Mr. F." – a compromise, how's that? Anyway, down there, I didn't *get* your music, you know what I'm saying? Up here, however, I *am* learning the finer things. I'm fooling around with *Cosi Fan Tutte* at the moment. A toughie!

HE *laughs again.*

Oh, that Howie! That rascal! You've been had, Mr. F. You have been royally *had*!

BRYCE: *(Scornfully)* You'll forgive if I don't share your enjoyment. As for "fooling around" with *Cosi Fan Tutte*, that hardly seems an appropriate posture, does it!

MOZART: Why the big bug up your – oh, sorry. Why are you so sore? Because you got scammed on your first day? It happens all the time!

BRYCE: Really!

MOZART: Yes, really! See, for every 445 days in attendance here, we earn one "scam option." For every 637 days in attendance, we earn one "revenge option." In your case, Howie used his "scam option," I think.

BRYCE: Scams? Revenges! In Heaven? I'm to *swallow* this?

MOZART: Even Heaven must have its safety valves, Mr. F.

BRYCE: Safety valves!

MOZART: Sure! Think of it this way, friend. New York has graffiti, yes? Denmark has Tivoli Gardens, they call it. Or is it Norway? I never remember. Colleges do beer parties, yes? Safety valves.

Escape hatches. We need them, too. Howie's had more than 445 days, many more, so he's *entitled* to his scam, you see?

BRYCE: I do *not* see. I do *not* approve.

MOZART: Once you've been with us a while, when all the blandness and the peace and quiet get to you, you *will* see, you *will* approve.

Aware now that BRYCE *is preparing to leave.*

Oh, don't go! Listen, *that* Mr. Mozart has already had his luncheon. And he dines alone, anyway. So, *sit*, my friend. I'll show you some of the ropes. Besides – no dinner. Remember?

Finally persuaded, BRYCE *sits, but doesn't touch his food.*

So! What did you give Howie?

BRYCE: What makes you think I gave him anything?

MOZART: It's the way the scams work. To be seated with *that* Mr. Mozart, you gave him maybe– ?

BRYCE: I don't care to discuss it.

MOZART: Okay by me, friend. Our best scammers? They settle for a marijuana cigarette or two, nothing more. I take that back. They *do* seem to be getting cheekier these days – wedding rings, neck chains–

BRYCE *bites his lip.*

What? You gave him something *valuable*?

BRYCE: I gave him…I gave him – never mind.

Now the celestial chimes ring again, BRYCE *wincing at the final note.* MOZART *looks at his monitor, smiles, pats it fondly, and puts it away.*

What *is* that frightful sound?

MOZART: You got a monitor, didn't you?

BRYCE *holds out his monitor.*

It hasn't rung yet?

BRYCE *shakes his head.*

Two sons just prayed for me. Whenever someone prays for you, it rings and you get a point. If you win the tally–

BRYCE: If you *what*?

MOZART: Whoever gets the most points by 3 PM wins a nice surprise.

BRYCE: The nice surprise might start with *playing* correctly!

MOZART: The Training Department is breaking in some new cherubs, that's all. A little patience, yes?

BRYCE: This is insane. This is *all* insane!

MOZART: No: it's just *new* to you. You'll get the hang of it.

HE *moves* BRYCE'S *tray closer to him.*

Eat. Please?

BRYCE: *(Glaring at* MOZART *a moment, then beginning to pick at his food)* If you're not *that* Mr. Mozart, what Mr. Mozart are you?

MOZART: Mo-*zart*. What Mr. Mo-*zart* are you! I could tell you, but I'm not sure I would do it *well*.

BRYCE: And why is that?

MOZART: After 926 days, we earn temporary bragging rights. I'm a real old-timer so I have *forever* bragging rights.

BRYCE: Try reining yourself in.

MOZART: It'll be hard.

Clearing his throat.

I am the Maurice Mo-*zart* affectionately known as Moe Mo-*zart* of "Mo-*zart*'s Beaux Arts." You've heard of it?

BRYCE: Hardly!

MOZART: You've been to urban bakeries?

BRYCE: A baker? A man with forever bragging rights is a *baker?*

MOZART: I am and then again, I am not. Think, Mr. F.: at urban bakeries, you've looked in the windows, perhaps? Seen the cakes, perfect cakes, *permanent* cakes, the ones that don't get stale and never spoil or melt in the sun? Mo-*zart*'s Beaux Arts at your service! I *made* those permanent cakes. I *manufactured* those permanent cakes!

BRYCE: What???

MOZART: Mo-*zart*'s Beaux Arts to the rescue, always! Waste? Never! Money down the drain? Forget it! Instead: Styrofoam molds, extruded novelties, masterpieces to dazzle the eye and whet the appetite. Florettes, garlands, imaginative patterns in glistening, color-fast pastels!

BRYCE: What????

MOZART: I am trying to tone down the self-promotion here, but you see how difficult it is.

BRYCE: What????

MOZART: *What*, all these "whats!" I'm talking captivating cakes in fancy display cases, seizing the attention week after week, month after month, year after year, always gorgeous, always enticing, most designed – exclusively, of course, by Mrs. Maurice Mo-*zart* herself. A lovely lady with a gift for lacy ornament. Yes! Designed by Mrs. Mo-*zart*, executed by Mo-*zart* and Sons. Achievements, Mr. F., achievements!

BRYCE: Achievements! False cakes?

MOZART: Exactly!

BRYCE: Achievements? Extruded novelties?

MOZART: Precisely!

BRYCE: Achievements? Mediocrities, you mean!

MOZART: That shows what *you* know. I'm talking the best in the industry. Vanilla? Hacks can do vanilla. Chocolate? A piece of cake, pardon the pun. I'm talking maple cream with marzipan clusters and marigold florettes! I'm talking poetry in the display case!

BRYCE: I am actually having a conversation with a manufacturer of... of phony baloney cakes! It's – impossible! It's – ludicrous! It's – mortifying!

MOZART: Nice words, all. But you think they curl themselves, the garlands? You think they shape themselves, the green leaves, the delicate vines and the tinted petals and the icy trims designed by my fair lady, then striated, combed? Look at my business card.

BRYCE: Why in the world would I–

MOZART: *(Reading from business card)* "We Put The Art in Artificial." Catchy, yes? My eldest wrote that! He has the gift.

BRYCE: I may be losing my mind. That is a *distinct* possibility.

MOZART: Oh, yes, friend, I went around the world for the finest materials, the gums, the resins, the polyesters, the lacquers. To Belgium. To Africa. To Greenland once. I didn't linger. Do you know how cold it is there?

BRYCE: I *have* lost my mind! That's it! I *lost* it on my way here!

MOZART: So snooty! Such a nose in the air! Such *pride*! "Hubris," those Greeks on the next mountain call it. To dismiss a good living from a valuable product, a real moneymaker! My sons continue a thriving business. My wife remains well-provided for. An entire family, connected to such excellence, pursuing it together! A happy life force, Mr. F.! But perhaps I am being insufferable?

BRYCE: You passed that threshold several paragraphs back.

MOZART: *(A bit more subdued)* I lived richly, that's why. Not to beat around the bush, I do very well up here, too. I conduct classes every afternoon in the creation of phony baloney cakes, as you choose to call them. What do you think of *them* apples?

BRYCE: *(Mostly to himself)* No, my mind is still functioning. It's a test of some sort, that's all. Yes! It's a controlled academic study, testing my tolerance of – of banality!

MOZART: Which classes are very well attended. What do you think of *them* apples?

BRYCE: *(Again, mostly to himself)* No, that is *not* it! I see it now! For some unimaginable reason, I have been consigned to the heaven from hell! Yes, that's it! The heaven from hell!

MOZART: Did *you* live richly, Mr. F.?

BRYCE: What? Of course, I lived richly!

MOZART: You had a wife?

BRYCE: Unnecessary.

MOZART: You had children?

BRYCE: Unnecessary.

MOZART: No wife, no children. Sad, Mr. F.: wives and children are the best things down there.

BRYCE: To repeat, and in the absence of bragging rights, I felt no need.

MOZART: You felt no need?

BRYCE: One doesn't require others to compose good music. Quite the opposite. Unlike some mere manufacturers, who–

MOZART'S *monitor chimes again, the wrong note making* BRYCE *wince.*

The heaven from hell! There's the proof!

MOZART: Hey! If this keeps up, I'll win today! Excuse me.

Consulting the monitor, HE *smiles.*

Bless their hearts! Look! They're praying for me at the Red Cross. You've heard of the Red Cross?

BRYCE, *utterly miserable, can only hold his head.*

That business you dismiss? It gave me plenty of money for good works, too. For four straight years? I was the largest single donor to the Red Cross east of the Mississippi. Four straight years, if you please...until I was toppled from first place.

BRYCE: Mo-*zart*'s Beaux Arts toppled? How is it even possible?

MOZART: I was toppled by a TV producer from New York. I didn't mind. I bear no grudge.

BRYCE: And why is that?

MOZART: He was guilt-ridden, poor man. All that sitcom crap – oh, sorry – every day of his life. Who could stand it? I gladly deferred to him. I needed no further validation.

A ruminative beat.

And there you have it, Mr. F. Wife...children...success...I am *that* Mr. Mo-*zart*. You asked, I told. "Finito," as they say.

BRYCE: Not a moment too soon! Well, Mr. Mo-*zart*, I lack bragging rights as yet, but if this is a game of some sort, a one-upsmanship duel, understand that *you* are looking at someone who wrote music, *good* music, *real* music, a new work every year! What do you think of *them – those* apples?

MOZART: Every year a new work? This, too, is impressive.

BRYCE: Guilty as charged.

MOZART: You ate, drank, slept your music?

BRYCE: Guilty as charged.

MOZART: A *Cosi Fan Tutte* in your trunk, maybe?

BRYCE: Maybe.

MOZART: Tell me this, then: how come I never heard of you? Do you have a business card?

BRYCE: Certainly not.

MOZART: Why certainly not? Your music never went anywhere, have I got that right?

BRYCE: I don't think I will answer that!

MOZART: Are you *sure* you lived richly?

BRYCE: *Or* that!

MOZART: You'll forgive me, Mr. F., but to me your life sounds like an incomplete kind of life, an empty kind of life.

BRYCE: You are *no one* to judge! I have made it into heaven, haven't I?

MOZART: Not to put you down too much, but *all* composers, good and bad, even the ones who led an incomplete kind of life, come to heaven automatically. Composers and master plumbers. Also junior high school civics teachers. I don't know why.

BRYCE: I believe I shall finish my lunch elsewhere, thank you.

MOZART: Hum me a piece.

BRYCE: What?

MOZART: Hum a piece for me, Mr. Composer. We'll see if your work is noteworthy.

BRYCE: I will not.

MOZART: Or *not* noteworthy.

BRYCE: I will not!

MOZART: Or maybe – to quote someone we both know – only "mediocrity."

BRYCE: *You*, Mr. Mo-*zart*, are the mediocre one at this table, not me!

MOZART: We can let the nasty crack pass, Mr. F., but please, your grammar! Don't say "At this table, not me." Say "At this table, not *I*."

BRYCE: *(Standing up, prepared to go)* I did *not* give up my watch to be subjected to–

MOZART: Your *watch*! You gave up your watch to Howie! That devil! Oh, figuratively, of course! But *you*: I feel for anyone so easily taken in by–

BRYCE *can take no more. But trying to exit,* HE *tips over his tray. In total frustration now,* HE *puts his hands over his face and sits again.*

Picking up a muffin from the floor.

I've been rough on you, too rough. And boastful. *And* arrogant. Would you allow me to apologize for these faults?

Brushing off the muffin with his sleeve.

Please: the muffin at least? It's okay, I promise. That's one thing in this place – the floors are spotless, guaranteed. Please?

Prying BRYCE'S *fingers from his face.*

Please?

Holding out the muffin again, even as BRYCE *refuses it.*

I take it all back, truly. *Everything.* I do. I sound off about my cakes all the time, but let's face it: Rembrandts they're not. And as for your watch, look at it this way: there is no need for a timepiece up here, am I right?

BRYCE: *(Subdued and mumbling)* Then why did Howie want it?

MOZART: Interesting, isn't it? The many ways of heaven, who can know? Anyway, like I was saying, my cakes are nothing, *nothing* next to your achievement, *nothing* next to winning a fine watch in a musical competition!

BRYCE: *(Looking* MOZART *straight in the eye)* I never told you that.

MOZART: I surmised. Did I surmise correctly?

BRYCE: The watch was a Rolex.

MOZART: What?

BRYCE: It was a *Rolex.*

MOZART: A Rolex! Some piece of goods, that! Couldn't you have given Howie-the-rascal something else?

BRYCE: It's the only thing I had.

MOZART: Ah.

BRYCE: At the accident scene, it was my last instruction: "Make sure my Rolex is still on my wrist, officer."

MOZART: Ah. I *do* understand.

BRYCE: You *can't* understand. It wasn't just a competition. It was a *major* competition. Forty entrants, all big talents.

MOZART: I *do* understand.

BRYCE: You *can't* understand. How could a manufacturer understand a composer's reason for living?

MOZART: The way a composer could understand a manufacturer's reason for living. Touché?

BRYCE: Touché.

MOZART: Good. Maybe now you'll take a bite?

BRYCE: *(Wistfully, anger subsiding)* Eating a muffin, scooped up from the floor, across a bistro table from a man named Mozart, who is *not* Mozart!

MOZART: Also interesting! No end of surprises, is there! Still, you have to admit–

THEY *are interrupted by the first notes of a song, "Bei Mir Bist Du Schoen." * THE TRIO *appears, pulling a small wagon, which contains a big net bag of tangerines, a gift certificate and a Thighmaster. * THE TRIO *places the gifts before* MOZART.

For me? Did I win today?

THE TRIO *nods in unison.*

Mr. F., do you see? It's *me*! Those Red Cross folks put me over!

ONE OF THE TRIO *reaches behind* MOZART'S *head. Suddenly his halo lights up: a neon circle of vibrant magenta.*

Concurrently, THE TRIO *serenades him, singing "Bei Mir Bist Du Schoen" in the style perfected by the Andrews Sisters of long ago.*

Finished, THE TRIO *kisses* MOZART *and, waving, leaves with the wagon.*

Didn't I tell you? Didn't I say? That was so nice! Wasn't that nice!

BRYCE: *(Strangely subdued)* It was *very* nice, Mr. Mo-*zart.*

MOZART: Who could ask for more, answer me that! Three pretty girls, a terrific song, a classic almost, if you'll pardon an old man's nostalgia. A lit-up halo, a gift certificate for 10 tango lessons, and my all-time favorite fruit! Also, in the bargain, a Thighmaster! Although–

Lowering his voice.

I didn't want to hurt their feelings, but *you* may have the Thighmaster if you want–

Now HE *sees the great pain building in* BRYCE.

What's the matter? What is it, Mr. F.?

BRYCE *does not answer. Instead,* HE *shakes his monitor violently, willing it to ring. But it does NOT ring.* HE *throws it to the ground.*

Softly

Nobody has prayed for you yet? *Nobody?*

BRYCE *shakes his head.*

A contest winner over 39 other entrants? How can that be?

HE *picks up the monitor and gently replaces it around* BRYCE'S *neck.*

Somebody *will* pray for you. I *know* they will.

BRYCE: Why should they?

MOZART: Why? What a question! You're a deserving person, that's why. You *are.* I say that without fear of contradiction.

BRYCE: You don't know.

MOZART: I *do* know! Your monitor didn't ring today, so what? Does that mean it won't ring tomorrow? It does *not!* You might get a prayer, a *long* one, at any time!

BRYCE: You don't know.

MOZART: I *do* know! Did I mention that any prayer over 3.6 minutes gets you *two* points? In a flash, you could be a contender!

BRYCE: *(Quietly)* Mr. Mo-*zart*: I didn't win that Rolex.

MOZART: You didn't?

BRYCE: I stole it.

MOZART: You stole it?

BRYCE: I stole it.

MOZART: You didn't merely – borrow it? You *stole* it?

BRYCE: I stole it from the contest winner.

MOZART: I suggest, right about now, that we eat some tangerines, yes?

BRYCE: I entered the competition with the best piece I ever wrote.

MOZART: Or use the Thighmaster. Why let it sit there?

BRYCE: I was *sure* I would win, absolutely sure! And I made the final cut, Mr. Mo-*zart*, I did!

MOZART: An achievement, if I ever heard one!

BRYCE: I was seated at the dais with 5 other finalists.

MOZART: Another achievement! I myself have *never* been seated at a dais!

BRYCE: Third prize winner was named. I wasn't concerned. "Let him have his $100 prize," I thought. "*I* will win."

MOZART: Listen, Mr. F.–

BRYCE: Second prize winner was named. I wasn't concerned. "Let him have his $500 prize," I thought. "*I* will win!"

MOZART: Yes, but listen, Mr. F.–

BRYCE: When they got to the first prize, I *knew* it would be me. I *knew*! I stood up before they even announced the name. And then...then...I couldn't believe my ears! It was...it was someone else's name they called.

MOZART: A major disappointment, I'm sure, but listen, Mr. F.–

BRYCE: He went to the judges' panel to claim his prize: the $1,000 check and...and...

MOZART: And the Rolex watch.

BRYCE: He put the check and the watch down on the table. A circle surrounded him, everyone crowding, offering congratulations, admiring him, applauding him, *loving* him. I watched. I watched a long time. Nobody was looking my way.

MOZART: Temptations, Mr. F.; temptations abound.

BRYCE: I didn't care about the check. I wasn't in it for the check.

MOZART: You were a finalist, Mr. F.... shouldn't that have counted for something?

BRYCE: It should have. But it didn't. I wanted...I wanted...

MOZART: Affirmation.

BRYCE: Yes. Affirmation. I wanted...I wanted...

MOZART: Validation.

BRYCE: Yes. Validation.

A painful beat.

I put my briefcase on the table.

MOZART: The watch went home with you.

BRYCE: Yes. The watch went home with me.

MOZART: As that Martha Stewart person might say, that was not a good thing.

BRYCE: No. That was not a good thing.

MOZART: *(A long beat)* But you wrote *more* music, Mr. F.

BRYCE *nods.*

Good music?

BRYCE *shrugs.*

Still, you *tried.* You *did* try, and that *does* count for something. It's why you're up here, I would bet my life on it!

BRYCE: *(Smiling sadly)* All composers and master plumbers and junior high school civics teachers. You told me yourself.

MOZART: But I don't always get things right. See, I don't hear that well–

BRYCE: Nice try, Mr. Mo-*zart.*

MOZART: I'll tell you what I think. I think this is not unfixable. If I may be so bold, you have some dues to pay, that's all.

BRYCE: Another nice try, Mr. Mo-*zart.*

MOZART: No, *listen* for once! We all lose our way sometimes. A superior person like yourself–

BRYCE: *You're* not the mediocre one at this luncheon. *I* am.

Smiling sadly.

Mo-*zart's* Beaux Arts topples phony baloney composer.

A long beat.

MOZART: I am having a most provocative thought! Let me share it with you, yes?

No response from BRYCE.

Not to beat a dead horse, friend, but was that Rolex watch by any chance *engraved*? You know, an inscription? A name? Anything?

A shrug from BRYCE.

I mean, the lucky composer who won: who was he? It was a long time ago, I know, but – any clue?

Another shrug from BRYCE.

Was it…could it have been…was the lucky composer named – Mr. Stratton?

BRYCE: I don't know. I can't recall.

MOZART: Think, Mr. F., *think*! Couldn't it…could it have been a man named Mr. Howard Stratton?

BRYCE: I draw a blank, Mr. Mo-*zart*. Unless–

MOZART: A provocative thought, "unless." Unless – ?

BRYCE: Unless…there were initials on the back of the case, I remember. Yes: three engraved initials. What were they?

MOZART: "HRS," perhaps?

BRYCE: I don't really…Yes! "HRS!" How did you know?

MOZART: A surmise. A good surmise! Oh, that rascal! That scamp! He's a real pisser, that one! Oh, sorry.

BRYCE: Howie?

MOZART: Full name: Howard R. Stratton. Do you *believe* the man! He used both his "scam option" *and* his "revenge option" at the same time! Simultaneously, as it were! After all these years, the watch returns to the correct wrist! Doesn't that make you feel better? It *should*! How do you feel? Better?

BRYCE: As a matter of fact, I do.

MOZART: Maybe even a little – glad?

BRYCE: Yes! I *am* glad!

MOZART: Paid in full! Account satisfied! Symmetry!

BRYCE: Symmetry?

MOZART: Revenge? His. Sweet! Redemption? Yours. Also sweet! Symmetry!

BRYCE: Symmetry, indeed.

MOZART: Even in heaven, we can't do much about those *big* things – you know, death and taxes, airplane crashes and holocausts – but we *do* manage to level things out a little bit. I like to call it "semi-intelligent design."

HE *makes a balancing gesture with his hands.*

You've had a rough day, Mr. F. A little reward, maybe? How would you like to meet *your* Mr. Mozart? The real one, the Wolfgang Amadeus one!

BRYCE: You could do that?

MOZART: There's a semi-chance.

BRYCE: You *know* him?

MOZART: I can't be said to *know* him. No one really *knows* him. But most days he attends my class.

HE *reaches under the table for an artificial cake.*

I made this for him, actually. A beauty, you'll agree.

BRYCE: You'd bring that to *him*?

MOZART: It's my world famous maple cream.

BRYCE: Yes, but it's so…so…unlikely!

MOZART: What is unlikely about it? He likes deconstructing my cakes. He'll have a ball with this one.

BRYCE: *(In no way hostile as before)* "Deconstructing." You don't *mean* "deconstructing" your cakes?

MOZART: I mean deconstructing my cakes! He's not very good at it, but I'm a patient fellow.

BRYCE: You'll forgive me, please, but this is a bit hard to take.

MOZART: What's hard? I'm deconstructing *Cosi Fan Tutte*, aren't I? That last scene? It's a doozie! For 217 years, no one's understood what's going on in that last scene! Who knows? I may be the one to sort it out for Mr. M.!

BRYCE: *(Musing)* Artificial maple cream cake, deconstructed by Mozart. *Cosi Fan Tutte*, deconstructed by Mo-*zart*'s Beaux Arts. Symmetry?

MOZART: Symmetry!

HE *rises to start out.*

Now: a few instructions. Mr. Mozart will wave to me, but not to you. On a good day, he will wave like this–

HE *demonstrates a wave.*

Then we can approach him. If he doesn't, well, we wait till next time. Also, you must remember to laugh at his jokes. He likes it if you laugh at his jokes. Not a squeaky little giggle, not a paltry chortle, but a guffaw. Like this–

HE *demonstrates a guffaw.*

You hear what I'm saying?

Suddenly a monitor rings.

BRYCE: Not again! Somebody *please* get those cherubs on key!

HE *notices that it is his monitor.*

Hey! It's *my* monitor! *My* monitor rang!

HE *consults his monitor again.*

You! You prayed for me!

MOZART: Why not?

BRYCE: When? *When* did you?

MOZART: When you were telling about the – you know.

HE *points to his wrist.*

It wasn't a *long* prayer. Not to spoil you right off, you know? But it's a start, yes?

BRYCE: A wonderful start.

MOZART: It took them long enough to register the prayer, but your records probably aren't in the files yet.

BRYCE: I *am* beholden to you, Mr. Mo-*zart*. I am *much* beholden to you.

MOZART: Hey! I am having another provocative thought. *You're* the one to get those cherubs on key, maybe?

BRYCE: Maybe. Maybe I am.

MOZART: Good! Now hurry: I'm not there on time, the class throws spitballs; I kid you not. And Wolfgang leads the pack!

BRYCE: Mr. Mo-*zart*? That magnificent maple cream cake? May I carry it for you?

MOZART: Sure!

HE *gives* BRYCE *the cake.*

Now, remember–

BRYCE: I know. Not a squeaky giggle, not a paltry chortle, but a guffaw. Like *this*–

HE *demonstrates a guffaw as he and* MOZART *go off together.*

THE CURTAIN FALLS
END OF PLAY

THE VISITING ROOM

a one-act play

The Visiting Room

production history:

In April 1997, this play was presented by Corner Loft Studios at the Harold Clurman Theatre, New York City, as part of the 22nd Annual Samuel French One-Act Play Festival. A Critics' Choice selection, it was given an added performance. It was directed by Richard Shepard with the following cast:

Margaret . . . . .Anne-Marie Caron
Gordon . . . . Don Berry
Pauline . . . . Elaine Gold
Attendant . . . . David Saltzman

In February 2001, this play was presented jointly by Stageplays Theatre Company and the Episcopal Actors' Guild at Guild Hall, New York City. It was directed by Tom Ferriter with the following cast:

Margaret . . . . Kit Flanagan
Gordon . . . . .Peter Von Berg
Pauline . . . . Evelyn Page
Attendant . . . . Rebecca Johnson

setting:

The interior of a well-appointed nursing home. It is *not* a depressing place; it has won architectural awards. It expresses affluence...and guilt.

time:
The present, Sunday afternoon.

characters:
DORETTA, the aide, maybe 20 or 25

PAULINE, the mother, 70

MARGARET, the wife, about 50

GORDON, the husband, about 50

AT RISE: PAULINE *dozes in her wheelchair, purse clutched above her blanket.*

DORETTA, *the aide, enters with grooming items on a tray.* DORETTA *is a good-natured and good care-giver. We won't ever know how much of her soothing chit-chat reaches* PAULINE.

DORETTA: *(Quietly touching* PAULINE'S *cheek)* Come, darlin'. Time.

PAULINE, *eyes still shut, opens her mouth automatically.*

No, darlin'. No pills yet. We got to make you pretty.

PAULINE *pushes her off.*

Oh, now, darlin': you're not mad at Doretta today. You know you're not. Give us a kiss and we will forget it, okay?

SHE *kisses* PAULINE.

First, we're going to comb this lovely hair.

SHE *sets about doing so.*

It *is* Sunday, and it *is* close to 5 o'clock, darlin', nearly time for the big show. That's right, my precious, *show* time!

A beat as SHE *works.*

She'll come first, your daughter-in-law, want to bet? Dressed fit for the Opera?

Imitating

"Hello, Pauline. Doretta, isn't it?"

A wince from PAULINE.

Too tight, darlin'? I am sorry. She'll wear those understated pearls today, don't you think? I think *yes.* I do love understated pearls, don't you, darlin'?

A beat as SHE *works.*

Then *he'll* come, won't he, the loving ha, ha! son, and we know what *he'll* be wearin'! Understated guilt!

Laughing at her own joke, getting no response from PAULINE.

The Sunday Afternoon Big Show! Just for your benefit, except we know better, don't we, darlin'? It's for *her* benefit.

Putting toilet water on PAULINE'S *arms.*

Now, nothing's to upset you, you hear me? I'll be right outside.

SHE *sniffs* PAULINE'S *arms.*

There, now. Aren't you the pretty pumpkin! A sweet, pretty, jasmine pumpkin!

Through a plate glass window, we see MARGARET, *50, crossing the court toward the entrance door.* DORETTA *is dead right about her:* SHE *is understated, cool and classy.* SHE *carries a purse and a small ribboned package.*

Turning PAULINE'S *wheelchair.*

Here she comes, darlin', right on time! Red suit, red shoes, red purse, dyed in the same vat, darlin', which does not come cheap.

Laughing

Look! The pearls!

MARGARET *disappears for a moment from the plate glass.*

Taking PAULINE'S *face tenderly.*

You going to be good? You going to talk? You *can*!

There is no response.

Here's your blackboard. Here's your chalk.

PAULINE *would throw the blackboard to the floor, but* DORETTA *saves it just in time.*

This is *Doretta*, love!

At PAULINE'S *continued adamance.*

Okay, then, let's have the chalk.

But PAULINE *will not give it up.*

Darlin', ain't no use to have chalk if there's no blackboard.

But PAULINE *will not give up the chalk. Resignedly,* DORETTA *puts the blackboard on the table.* SHE *looks at her watch. Then, imitating again.*

"Hello, Pauline. Doretta, isn't it?" *Now*!

MARGARET: *(Entering)* Hello, Pauline. Doretta, isn't it?

DORETTA: Look, love, you're first today with a visitor. It's Margaret. Isn't that nice?

MARGARET: How are you feeling, Pauline?

DORETTA: She is *not* speaking with us today. She gets this way, lately, if she naps too long.

MARGARET: But she is all right?

DORETTA: Would you like to take her into the court?

Leaning into PAULINE'S *ear.*

It's a beautiful afternoon. You want to go outside?

There is no response.

She *is* having a day.

MARGARET: I know those days.

PAULINE *now makes a sign: two fingers at the mouth.*

DORETTA: No, love. You had my last one, you know that.

SHE *holds out her empty pack for* MARGARET'S *possible help.*

She does like her cigarettes, still.

MARGARET: I've given up smoking, I'm afraid.

DORETTA: See how smart Margaret is? She has given up smoking!

To MARGARET

She'll forget in a minute. You'll ring, if there's something she needs?

SHE *presses a buzzer on the table.* SHE *has given this demonstration before.*

MARGARET: *I'll* take care of her.

DORETTA: There, you see? Margaret will take care of you.

MARGARET: Have you seen Mr. Waring, Doretta? Earlier this week, perhaps?

DORETTA *shakes her head.*

He'll come today, then.

DORETTA: Are you and Mr. Waring going to eat with us tonight?

MARGARET: I imagine.

DORETTA: Are you and Mr. Waring going to get together again?

MARGARET: I don't think that's a question for you to ask, do you?

DORETTA: (SHE *has stepped over a line and knows it.* SHE *concentrates on* PAULINE) I'll be back in a few minutes with your pills.

Adjusting the blanket.

Feet warm? Diaper dry?

SHE *bends closer to* PAULINE.

Don't let them get to you, now. Just enjoy the show.

SHE *exits.*

MARGARET: *(Perfunctorily)* What show is that, Pauline?

Alone with PAULINE, *her actions are very guarded. No responses are forthcoming from* PAULINE, *of course.*

I was here last Sunday, do you remember? Just about this time?

A beat

Gordon missed last Sunday. Do you have any idea why?

A beat. SHE *offers the blackboard.*

Please: can't you talk? *Won't* you talk?

SHE *puts the blackboard down.*

I brought you something.

SHE *gets the package and puts it on* PAULINE'S *lap. The immediate response:* PAULINE *knocks it to the floor.*

Please don't act like this. Please?

SHE *picks up the package and unwraps it. It is a framed picture, which* SHE *puts on* PAULINE'S *lap. The immediate response:* PAULINE *knocks it to the floor. This time, the glass cracks.*

Now see what you've done.

A controlled MARGARET *picks up the picture and puts it on a table.* SHE *moves the wheelchair to the side of the room, punishing* PAULINE *as a child might be punished, with isolation.*

If you act like a child, Pauline, you'll be treated like one.

MARGARET *goes to the other side of the room.* SHE *takes a mirror and lipstick from her purse.* PAULINE *mimics these actions with her chalk, placing it in her purse when* MARGARET *completes the touch-up.*

MARGARET *does not immediately see the visitor coming into view in the court. It is* GORDON, *about 50, carrying a small plant.* HE *is ordinary, bland, unassuming.* DORETTA *has been, though, dead wrong about him: his guilt is, if anything, overstated. If* MARGARET *gives the appearance of total control, his shaky balance can be undone readily.*

HE *is about to disappear from momentary view when* MARGARET *spots him.* SHE *is suddenly interested in* PAULINE *again, picking up the picture and going to her, turning the wheelchair and bending patiently before it.*

I found it this morning, Pauline, just this morning.

Pointing to the picture.

There's Gordon. There *I* am. Who's the little girl, do you think? That's right! Christy! Your granddaughter, Christy! She'd come to see you, but her work has taken her miles and miles away.

A beat

She was so tiny, then. We were in Bermuda that year. A boy at the hotel took the picture. Gordon's holding her hand so tightly, see? Because the waves were so high!

GORDON: *(Who has seen this tender exchange, as he was meant to see it, from the doorway)* Hello, Margaret.

MARGARET: *(Standing)* Hello, Gordon.

GORDON: How are you today, Mother?

There is no response.

I brought this for you. Do you like it?

There is no response. PAULINE *is just about to throw it from her lap when* GORDON *saves it, laughing.*

MARGARET: Doretta said she napped too long.

GORDON: Is that right, Mother? You napped too long?

MARGARET: One of those days, Doretta said. But she's fine.

GORDON: Is that right, Mother? One of those days?

HE *puts the plant down.*

I guess it is.

MARGARET: Are you well, Gordon?

GORDON: *(Nodding)* Are you?

MARGARET: Yes.

GORDON: What have you been doing with yourself?

MARGARET: End-of-term. You remember what that's like.

GORDON: I remember, yes.

A beat

You are continuing with piano?

MARGARET *nods.* HE *smiles.*

The piano light still throwing off entirely too much heat?

MARGARET *nods.*

Break down and buy a new one.

MARGARET: I never seem to get around to it.

GORDON: You look nice in that color. But then – you always look nice.

MARGARET: I think bright colors are good for *her.*

GORDON: Is that right, Mother?

HE *crosses to the TV set and turns it on. There is reflected light from the picture, but no sound.*

There's still no sound. Why don't they repair the damn thing!

MARGARET: There are other sets around the place, Gordon.

GORDON: That doesn't mean they can't fix this one.

To PAULINE

You want to watch TV, Mother? There's no sound, but TV is better that way, take my word.

MARGARET: So cynical, Gordon! A sea change: I don't recall your being cynical.

GORDON: Was I being cynical? I was trying to be clever. But then – I never could tell the difference.

MARGARET: We shouldn't be *either.* For *her* sake.

GORDON: *(Turning off the set)* It doesn't seem to matter one way or the other.

MARGARET: She senses more this month than last. I *believe* that.

GORDON: You're being very concerned. I don't recall you were ever so concerned about her.

MARGARET: She wasn't so needy then.

GORDON: I thought you didn't *like* my mother, Margaret.

MARGARET *would protest.*

Oh, don't worry about it.

MARGARET: I *did* like her. I *do* like her.

GORDON: *(To* PAULINE*)* You hear that, Mother? Margaret did like you and does like you.

Noticing the picture.

Where did this come from?

MARGARET: I was rearranging some things in the closet.

GORDON: The Bahamas?

MARGARET: Bermuda.

GORDON: Christy was so little. I'd forgotten. How *is* Christy?

MARGARET: Surely she's in touch?

GORDON: Not noticeably.

MARGARET: She's busy with her work, I imagine.

GORDON: It wasn't that much better before she went out there.

MARGARET: She's puzzled by you still, I suppose.

GORDON: That makes two of us. *I'm* puzzled by me still. How did the glass get broken?

MARGARET: It was broken when I found it.

GORDON: *She* threw it to the floor.

MARGARET: *(Coolly)* It was broken when I found it.

Now PAULINE *starts to gesture that she would like a cigarette.*

I'm sorry, Pauline. You know I don't smoke any more.

GORDON: You've quit, Margaret! Good for you!

MARGARET: I don't even need to have them with me any more.

GORDON: Then these months – they've been good for you?

MARGARET: *(Laughing)* Is that what you think? Is that what you *want* to think? Not so! For weeks after you…after you left, I found myself smoking entirely too much. It took time to realize what I was doing to myself, but I came to my senses.

Pointedly

We all come to our senses, eventually.

GORDON: *(A beat: he's not biting)* You do have enough money?

MARGARET: Have I asked for money?

GORDON: If you *didn't* have enough, you wouldn't ask me.

MARGARET: *(Patting* PAULINE'S *hair)* He likes my suit, Pauline. He likes my discipline. He likes my independence. There's hope for me yet.

To GORDON

Or would your friend – what's her name, Karen? – object to my saying so?

GORDON: That doesn't become you, Margaret.

MARGARET: I suppose it doesn't. Still – sometimes I feel I didn't fight hard enough to have you stay.

GORDON: Put the picture away.

MARGARET: I *thought* I had fought hard enough.

GORDON: Put the goddamn picture away!

MARGARET: Didn't I fight hard enough, Gordon?

GORDON: *(Putting the picture face down and abruptly returning to* PAULINE'S *wheelchair)* They know visitors will come. Why don't they keep her from napping too long!

MARGARET: They can't *know* visitors will come.

GORDON: It's Sunday, isn't it? It's 5 o'clock, isn't it?

MARGARET: You're not here every Sunday. You weren't here last Sunday.

GORDON: *(With mounting anger)* But you were. Am I right? Last Sunday? Like the Sunday before? Like the Sunday before that?

MARGARET *has spotted* DORETTA *in the doorway, with her tray of pills.* MARGARET *signals to* GORDON *to change his tone, but he does not notice.*

You come every goddamn Sunday at 5 o'clock, don't you? The question is: why?

MARGARET: Yes, Doretta?

GORDON: *(Hurriedly; shamedly)* Hello, Doretta.

DORETTA: *(Directing everything to* PAULINE*)* It's time, isn't it, love?

Kneeling before her with pills.

Are you having yourself a fine afternoon with your family?

GORDON: *(Trying to change his tone)* That TV set isn't working, Doretta. Oh, it's a small thing, I know. There are sets all around the place.

MARGARET: *(Kneeling beside the wheelchair)* So many pills, Doretta.

DORETTA: *(Feeding pills to* PAULINE*)* Good. Good.

MARGARET *helps by taking the tray.*

Thank you.

GORDON: *(Observing and knowing he should be part of the care, too)* Would $50 have it fixed? $100? My gift?

DORETTA: We got a new TV due in a week, Mr. Waring.

To PAULINE

Isn't that right, love?

MARGARET: *(Holding up pills)* And these?

DORETTA: This is for her pressure.

To PAULINE

We keep it nice and low, don't we, darlin', so Doctor won't fuss at us again?

GORDON: This is a nice enough place. As these places go, I mean.

DORETTA: We think so.

GORDON: You treat the patients well, don't you?

DORETTA: They're not our patients, Mr. Waring. They're our residents. They're our loves.

To PAULINE

She's my favorite, you know. And now – your tranquilizer.

To MARGARET *and* GORDON

It's very mild. It keeps her from becoming too agitated.

MARGARET: But it's not necessary today, is it?

DORETTA: It's better for her, Mrs. Waring, to stay on schedule.

MARGARET: She looks so good this afternoon. I think we should keep her alert. Don't you think so, too, Gordon?

There is no response from GORDON.

DORETTA: *(A beat)* We can let it wait till dinnertime. Shall I sign you up for dinners?

There is no response from GORDON.

MARGARET: Gordon?

DORETTA: Baked chicken leg tonight, and it *is* good. Visa accepted.

SHE *waits in vain for reaction to her little joke.*

I'll check with you later.

SHE *starts to exit.*

MARGARET: She seems so much better today. There is every reason to hope.

GORDON: *(Angry about two things now –* MARGARET'S *insistence on hope, and the caring* HE *has just seen, but which he can't feel or provide –* HE *stops* DORETTA *in her tracks)* Just why is she your favorite?

MARGARET: Gordon!

GORDON: I'm talking to you!

DORETTA: Me?

GORDON: I foot the bills. I want to know! She's only been here six weeks. Why is she your favorite?

DORETTA *moves* PAULINE *to a corner of the room, turning the wheelchair so that her back is to the audience.*

Trying to protect her from unpleasantness, SHE *touches* PAULINE'S *cheek and turns to face* GORDON.

DORETTA: Because, Mr. Waring, under this quiet, there is a heart. And a brain. It's forgotten how to do for itself most of the time, but it's there, all the same.

GORDON: A small heart. A crafty brain.

MARGARET: He doesn't mean that!

GORDON: A cunning brain, when it worked.

MARGARET: *(Stepping into the breach)* Gordon means only that she should be kept from napping too much, so she'll be more responsive with us.

GORDON: That is *not* what I mean.

MARGARET: I told him: you can't possibly know when visitors are coming.

GORDON: Don't apologize for me. I'll apologize for me.

To DORETTA

I apologize.

DORETTA: We try, Mr. Waring. We try.

SHE *gives the buzzer a short demonstration buzz.*

If you need me.

To PAULINE

Bye, love.

SHE *exits.*

GORDON: Why do you do that?

MARGARET: Why do I do what?

GORDON: Explain me. What I mean and what I don't mean. Why?

MARGARET: Why do you behave badly, so I have to explain?

GORDON: I don't know why.

He laughs.

Because we've always done it that way, I guess!

A beat

All those years, Margaret: I *did* try. I *have* tried.

MARGARET: *(Quietly)* I know.

GORDON: It stopped working. You *know* it stopped.

MARGARET: Yes.

GORDON: There was no point.

MARGARET: No point.

GORDON: We made each other unhappy.

MARGARET: And you're happy now?

GORDON: The lady asks a good question. Am I happy?

HE *sits down.*

Do you want me to be?

MARGARET: Of course.

GORDON: No, you don't.

MARGARET: My mistake.

GORDON: Maybe I *am* happy. Or maybe a little numb. A lot has happened lately, Margaret.

HE *opens his mouth, but closes it again:* HE *cannot bring himself to tell her yet.*

You do see people?

MARGARET: I see friends.

GORDON: You do go out sometimes? To dinner? To those concerts you like?

MARGARET: Do I date? Is that what you're asking me? I don't.

GORDON: Why not?

MARGARET: I think it's strange you'd ask.

GORDON: Why? Why strange? I've left, Margaret. I've left *you.*

MARGARET: Would you feel less guilty if I did the kind of thing you do?

GORDON: It's not necessary for any of us to feel guilty.

MARGARET: Even Karen? She of the firm body and the young skin and the brave talk, no doubt, about honest relationships? Shouldn't *she* feel guilty?

GORDON: We did *not* feel guilty, Margaret.

MARGARET: Most definitely my mistake.

GORDON: *(A beat. Then, quietly)* Why weren't *we* more interested in each other, do you suppose?

MARGARET: I was not uninterested. That's your fiction.

GORDON: *(Not listening; rather intent on his own thoughts)* It's not your fault. I'm not an interesting person. I don't read books. I don't like books. I don't look at paintings. I don't listen to music. I don't have vision, Margaret. You *thought* I did, but you should have been smart enough, from the beginning, to see I don't.

MARGARET: *(Laughing)* I made you feel unequal: is that what you'd like to think?

GORDON: Every night of my life with you, I risked condemnation.

MARGARET: I never condemned you.

GORDON: *I* condemned me. I'm a good plodder, that's what I am.

He goes to PAULINE.

Fourth from the bottom in my class, remember, Mother? But I was a good plodder, wasn't I? Careful? Correct? Thank God for a family business to hand down to your dull son, right, Mother?

Turning to MARGARET.

It has supported us well, Margaret, and all it takes is a little plodding!

MARGARET: I think sometimes you crave ordinariness, Gordon.

GORDON: *(Not listening)* Still: I've never missed a day. And I've made it grow. Those things should count for something.

MARGARET: They do.

GORDON: *(Not listening; pacing)* They should matter. Why don't they?

A defeated pause.

Things happen, that's why. Life happens. After a while, there's only accommodation. After another while, accommodation isn't enough.

Abruptly

You read too much, Margaret. Reading has nothing to do with the way people are or the way they feel.

MARGARET: How little you know me, Gordon.

GORDON: *(Sadly)* I do envy you – with your students! I remember, when you talked about them, or if I asked about them, there was something alive in your face, in your eyes, lighting them up.

MARGARET: I didn't think you noticed. Or understood.

GORDON: I noticed. I understood. Don't underestimate me. I'm not dumb.

MARGARET: I do not underestimate you, Gordon. That's another of your fictions.

GORDON: I never saw that look in your eyes for me.

MARGARET: I tried, too, Gordon.

GORDON: I know. I know that. It doesn't matter. Why are we letting it matter?

MARGARET: *(Daring to expose her vulnerability at last)* Gordon? I'm so very lonely. You can't know my loneliness.

GORDON: You said there were friends.

MARGARET: They're only friends.

GORDON: You have Christy.

MARGARET: I talk long-distance to Christy. I don't *have* Christy.

GORDON: You used to be so self-sufficient. That was the thing I admired most.

MARGARET: Was it? It's gone. It's crept off somewhere.

A beat

You can't know the loneliness in that apartment. It's the dinner-hour I dread most. The day has had no focus, I see then, and *won't* have. I feel so, so disconnected. It's a kind of sickness, Gordon. It ought to have a name. Dinner-hour loneliness!

A beat

Perhaps you're right. Perhaps I read too much.

GORDON: Now I'll tell you what I admired *least*, Margaret.

MARGARET: *(Caught up very short by the fact that* HE *hasn't seemed to hear her)* What?

GORDON: I admired least that you opened the living room windows before sitting down at the piano.

MARGARET *would protest.*

I know, I know: the piano light throwing off all that heat. Tell me the real reason. I want you to say it.

MARGARET: *(Quietly)* You haven't listened.

GORDON: You wanted to be *heard* at the piano.

MARGARET: You haven't listened to a word I said.

GORDON: Can't you admit it even now? "I want everyone in the building to hear me." Say it – just once.

MARGARET: I will not say it because it's not true.

GORDON: Forget it, then, Margaret.

Laughing

You see? It doesn't matter. It doesn't matter at all.

Exploding at PAULINE.

Mother, why are you like this? There is so much pain here, so much pain!

His face turns red. HE *sits down and covers it with his hands.*

MARGARET: Gordon?

GORDON: Why have you turned Christy against me?

MARGARET: I haven't.

GORDON: She won't even speak to me.

MARGARET: I never let what happened come between you. Give me credit for that much.

GORDON: *(Covering his face again)* She won't see me. She won't let me go out there to see her. I wanted...I wanted to meet her someplace, any place. I wanted...I wanted to explain what it means to me to try a new life.

A beat

She barely came to the phone. And then...and then...she said she doesn't ever want to see me again.

A long beat.

MARGARET: That happened – last week. Last Sunday.

GORDON *nods.* HE *will nod to each of her observations in this litany of observations.*

Of course, it was last Sunday. Afterwards, you took to your bed. You stayed there the rest of the day. You didn't eat. You *couldn't* eat. You didn't make it here, or anywhere. You slept. No: you *hid.* No sea change there, Gordon.

Coolly, delivering her thrust.

And that's the thing *I* admired least.

SHE *sits, her contempt spent.*

GORDON: *(A moment of silence. Then, marshalling his best defense mechanism – his anger – again,* HE *stands)* I know why *I* come here, Margaret. For the life of me, I can't figure out why *you* come.

MARGARET: You know why.

GORDON: No. *Not* for her.

MARGARET: You know very well why.

GORDON: She's not your mother. She's *my* mother.

MARGARET: You won't try. *One* of us has to try.

GORDON: Why don't you try on Thursday at 2 o'clock?... On Friday at 3 o'clock?

MARGARET: Because I have things to do.

GORDON: Things to do, yes.

MARGARET: Classes to prepare.

GORDON: Classes to prepare, yes.

MARGARET: End-of-term. You seem to forget.

GORDON: I do keep forgetting end-of-term.

MARGARET: A life to lead. Some sort of life to lead!

GORDON: A life to lead. While you're leading it, you could stop by here on Sunday at 4 o'clock, couldn't you?

MARGARET: That isn't a question. That's an accusation.

GORDON: You know what I think, Margaret? I think you come here on Sunday at 5 o'clock because *I* come here on Sunday at 5 o'clock.

MARGARET: For her.

GORDON: The bright colors are for me.

MARGARET: For *her.*

GORDON: The sweetness and light, the foolish talk of improvement, the false hope: they're for me.

MARGARET: FOR HER!

> PAULINE *is showing signs of agitation now.* SHE *waves her hand wildly, tracing patterns in the air.*

> GORDON *doesn't see this.* But MARGARET *uses the development to sidestep his accusations.* SHE *goes to* PAULINE *and takes her hand.*

GORDON: FOR ME! IT'S ALL FOR ME! You keep coming here, you keep *me* coming here – my God, you're trying to get me back. Why would you want to?

MARGARET: Get Doretta.

GORDON: *(To* PAULINE*)* Do you know me, Mother? You don't.

MARGARET: Don't frighten her. Press the buzzer.

GORDON: *(Quietly)* You won't know me tomorrow. You won't know me ever again.

> *Turning to* MARGARET.

It's all for *me.*

MARGARET: Press the buzzer, Gordon.

GORDON: She's bonkers, you hear?

> *To* PAULINE

You are bonkers, aren't you, Mother?

Back to MARGARET.

SHE IS BONKERS! IT'S ALL FOR ME!

MARGARET'S *response is to head for the buzzer. Suddenly,* GORDON *grabs her wrist.*

Say the colors are for me. Say you turned Christy from me.

MARGARET *contemptuously tries to get away and to the buzzer.* GORDON *grabs both her wrists now.*

Say you want to be heard at the piano. Say there's no hope for her. Say you *pretend* there's hope to keep me coming. Say you're here every Sunday for me. Say it's all for me!

MARGARET *does not wince, does not cry out, admits nothing.* SHE *pulls away from him and defiantly presses the buzzer. The sound fills the room as* THEY *stand glaring at each other. The sound finally brings* DORETTA *into the room.*

DORETTA: *(Entering)* What is it, love? What?

SHE *observes* PAULINE'S *tracings in the air and laughs.*

Is that all?

GORDON: *(Hurriedly)* I won't be staying for dinner, Doretta.

DORETTA: *(To* PAULINE*)* It's here someplace. I put it down myself.

GORDON: I have a lot to take care of, Doretta, things to do.

DORETTA: Here you are!

Having picked up the blackboard, SHE *gives it to* PAULINE.

GORDON: There are preparations to make, packing to do.

DORETTA: *(To either or both of them)* She wants to talk, that's all.

GORDON: A life to lead – to try to lead.

DORETTA: *(To* PAULINE*)* Now – where's your chalk?

GORDON: I won't be coming again.

GORDON *looks at* MARGARET, *to see if she has heard.* SHE *has, from his first exchange with* DORETTA. SHE *stands perfectly still, coming to grips with this new information.*

DORETTA: *(Reaching into* PAULINE'S *purse)* In here? Now how come Doretta knows that?

SHE *finds the chalk.*

You sly one!

SHE *gives the chalk to* PAULINE.

GORDON: I won't be coming back at all, Doretta.

DORETTA: *(Not really listening)* What's that, Mr. Waring?

GORDON: I'm leaving the city.

DORETTA: *(To PAULINE)* Yes, love? Which one do you want to talk to?

But PAULINE is already at work at the blackboard.

GORDON: I'm leaving the state.

DORETTA: Is that a fact?

GORDON: Leaving the city and the state, yes.

DORETTA: *(Finally acknowledging him, and standing)* I'm sorry to hear that, Mr. Waring.

GORDON: *(To MARGARET)* Margaret? Did you hear? I won't be coming here again.

MARGARET, *stunned by the news, stands motionless.* DORETTA, *stepping into the breach, is at the ready at* PAULINE'S *wheelchair.*

DORETTA: Come, love. It's too beautiful to stay indoors.

GORDON: *(Calmly now: everything is out of his system at last, and* HE *is under real control for the first time)* Don't take her, Doretta.

DORETTA: Please, Mr. Waring.

GORDON: I ought to say a proper goodbye.

DORETTA: Mrs. Waring?

There is no response from MARGARET.

GORDON: I *have* to say a proper goodbye, Doretta.

DORETTA *stands in place, unsure what to do.* SHE *goes to* PAULINE *and adjusts the blanket around her legs.*

DORETTA: You keep this blanket around your little tootsies, love, so you don't freeze all up, you hear?

With a last look at MARGARET, DORETTA *exits.*

GORDON: I didn't have the courage to tell you while we were alone, Margaret.

A beat

Did you hear me?

MARGARET: *(Quietly)* I heard nonsense.

GORDON: Everything's arranged for the end of the week.

MARGARET: Your business?

GORDON: I've sold the business.

MARGARET: Sold it.

GORDON: I need a fresh start, Margaret.

MARGARET: *(Her cool self-control is vanishing now)* The whole world needs a fresh start.

GORDON: I am sorry.

MARGARET: You'd cut yourself off from her?

GORDON: She doesn't know me.

MARGARET: From your daughter?

GORDON: She doesn't *want* to know me.

MARGARET: Wasn't it enough of a fresh start to leave me?

There is no response from GORDON.

Who decided these new things? *I* didn't. Karen: did she decide them for you?

GORDON: *(Quietly)* That's over, Margaret.

MARGARET: Over.

GORDON: For a while now.

MARGARET: You're not surprised? It couldn't last. I knew it. You knew it, too.

GORDON: Yes, I knew it.

MARGARET: I can't feel sorry for you, Gordon.

GORDON: I'm not asking you to.

MARGARET: Then *why* all this?

GORDON: *(Quietly)* There's someone else.

MARGARET: Someone else.

GORDON: Someone very nice.

MARGARET: Someone else. You *are* cutting a wide swath, aren't you!

GORDON: Don't, Margaret.

MARGARET: The relationships do get confusing, don't they? How is one to keep track?

GORDON: Please, don't.

MARGARET: Haven't I played a role in your life, in *hers*? Coming here? Caring? I–

A beat

Someone else. Do I get to know her name?

There is no response from GORDON.

DO I GET TO KNOW HER NAME?

GORDON: *(Quietly)* Edith.

MARGARET: Edith. And is Edith also very young? Does Edith make *you* feel very young?

GORDON: She's older than you are. She isn't as attractive, Margaret. She doesn't wear clothes the way you do. She's – rather plain.

MARGARET: Edith is plain. And what does Edith do?

GORDON: She sells lamps.

MARGARET: *(Laughing)* She sells lamps. At department stores.

GORDON: *To* department stores.

MARGARET: Edith sells lamps to department stores. And does Edith know about me?

GORDON: Yes.

MARGARET: And you've mapped out a future with her? You'll live together, in another city and another state?

GORDON *nods.*

How modern of you. *Another* sea change: I never thought of you as modern.

GORDON: We have a chance at life. I *want* it, Margaret.

MARGARET: A chance at life! You sound like one of the romantics in my class!

GORDON: *(Almost to himself)* I *can* make a woman happy!

MARGARET: *(Laughing)* An infantile romantic! You *fool* not to know it!

GORDON: I *need* to make a woman happy!

MARGARET: I don't believe there is such a person.

GORDON: *(Consulting his watch)* She'll be waiting outside for me now.

MARGARET: There is *no one* waiting outside.

Losing her self-control at last, growing progressively more desperate.

You *can't* go, Gordon. Your mother is showing improvement every day. She'll come home, you'll see.

GORDON: She is showing no improvement.

MARGARET: Your new affair won't last, either, Gordon. These things get shorter, that's all. There is hope for us.

GORDON: There is no hope, Margaret.

MARGARET: You said I wasn't interested in you. I can be. There is hope.

GORDON: There is no hope, Margaret.

MARGARET: This Edith – it will end just as the other one ended. You do see that? YOU DO SEE THAT?

GORDON *turns away from her.*

Look at me. *Look* at me! There is hope for us.

GORDON: There is no hope, Margaret.

MARGARET: Do you want me to beg? I'll beg.

GORDON: *(Suddenly, hugging her firmly to him)* I don't want you to beg. I want you to let me go.

MARGARET: THERE IS NO ONE WAITING FOR YOU OUTSIDE!

GORDON *breaks from her, and walks slowly to* PAULINE, *who is concentrating laboriously on her writing, as* SHE *will do throughout* GORDON's *farewell to her.*

GORDON: This is a nice place, isn't it, Mother? You do like it here?

A beat

They treat you well. You know they do.

A beat

I can't help you. You do see that?

A beat

I didn't mean the things I said before, Mother, but I won't be coming back again. Do you understand?

Of course, in all this, there has been no response from PAULINE.

Goodbye, Mother.

HE *kisses* PAULINE's *head. Then* HE *turns to* MARGARET.

Margaret? Your good wishes?

MARGARET *simply looks at him.*

You have mine.

HE *exits sadly.*

As PAULINE *writes on her blackboard,* MARGARET *stands motionless at the window. Through the plate glass, we see* GORDON *emerge from the building, walking dejectedly past the canopy, the railings.*

Now, suddenly, MARGARET *sees something we do not see. Is that* EDITH *walking somewhere in front of the building?*

MARGARET *watches for a long moment, back to the audience. Then her arms drop slowly in defeat.* SHE *turns from the window, her self-control returning.* SHE *crosses to her purse.* SHE *opens it and takes out a cigarette.*

PAULINE *immediately makes known her wish for a cigarette via the signal we saw earlier.* MARGARET *puts the cigarette into* PAULINE'S *mouth, puts another into her own mouth, and lights both their smokes.* PAULINE *returns to her chalking.*

DORETTA *appears at the doorway.* SHE *watches them for a moment. Taking two ashtrays from a drawer,* SHE *places them, one next to* MARGARET, *the other one on* PAULINE'S *lap.*

DORETTA: *(To* PAULINE*)* Smell that good baked chicken, love?

To MARGARET

Staying for dinner?

There is a long beat. MARGARET *looks at* DORETTA *blankly. Then, at last, because* SHE *still suffers from the dinner-hour loneliness* SHE *has described,* SHE *slowly nods.*

To PAULINE

There's going to be company for dinner. Isn't that nice?

PAULINE *continues to write on her blackboard.*

To MARGARET

You'll take her in?

MARGARET *nods. Her capitulation is complete.*

Flicking some ash from PAULINE'S *cigarette into the ash tray.*

There are good times, sometimes, aren't there, love!

SHE *exits.*

MARGARET: *(Ready to push the wheelchair)* Feet warm? Diaper dry?

As SHE *begins to move the wheelchair,* PAULINE *finishes her writing.* SHE *holds out the blackboard.*

MARGARET *takes it and reads.* SHE *laughs.*

Of course, you want to live. We *all* want to live.

MARGARET *is pushing the wheelchair as the lights dim.*

THE CURTAIN FALLS
END OF PLAY

ON A WEST SIDE ROOF, 1 IN THE AFTERNOON

a dramatic monologue

On A West Side Roof, 1 In The Afternoon

production history:

In May 2000, this play was presented by New York Playwrights Group at Center Stage, New York City. It was directed by Nina Steiger with the following cast:

Pegeen: . . . . Mary Unser

setting:

A not-very-glamorous rooftop.
Required props are 3 deck chairs, and a small pyramid of loose bricks.

time:

The present, daytime.

character:

PEGEEN
in her late thirties.
Alone on the stage, she will relate to four unseen people – her child, her mother, her neighbor, and her neighbor's child. Though unseen, these are *real* people; PEGEEN is *not* delusional.

AT RISE: The furnishings are 3 deck chairs, 2 side-by-side, the other a discreet distance away.

At the front of the stage is a small pyramid of loose bricks, which suggest the low parapet wall that surrounds the roof. They also suggest the need for repairs on this roof.

As the lights come up, PEGEEN *enters, juggling a cane, a tape recorder, a brown paper bag, and, most importantly, of course, her child in a white satin blanket.*

PEGEEN:

Now, Mother, you stay till I put all this down and settle our precious one, all right?

SHE *puts things down, especially careful with the child.*

There, my precious. Cozy?

SHE *rises and mimes helping her mother to a deck chair.*

Hold my hand, mother. You know, your limp is so much better? I believe it is going to leave us! Now! See how easy that was? We are nicely settled, the three generations, on this breezy roof, on this nice afternoon, *enjoying*!

SHE *looks toward the third deck chair.*

There is company today, Mother: that lady who just moved in below us. I'll say hello, okay? You *will* watch over our precious for a minute, won't you?…No, just one minute, Mother.

SHE *goes to the third deck chair.*

Hello, there. I'm going to introduce myself to you. I am Pegeen? On the floor just above you? And your name?…How do you do, then, Myra? It is nice to meet you…I have been dying to view *your* precious up close…Oh, sweet, sweet and smiley! And her name is?…Trisha. A lovely name for a lovely baby!… Mine? Mine is named Lizbeth, Baby Lizbeth, after my mother, Lizbeth…No, I'll let you see Baby Lizbeth *later*, if you don't mind, after I've explained about her a little…Well, yes, I *could* do that: I *could* get my chair and bring it over. I'll be right back.

SHE *returns to her own chair.*

Mother? I am going to chat a bit with our new neighbor. You'll keep a watchful eye, just one little, watchful eye, on our precious, won't you?…What? What *is* the problem? Mother, I will be right back! It's only common courtesy!…Mother, do *not* be selfish…Well, Mother, I am *going*, and that's all there is to that!

Louder now, so the neighbor will hear.

Thank you, Mother.

SHE *moves her deck chair to where the neighbor sits.*

There! I do feel I know you, Myra. From my door, which I leave open sometimes to catch a breeze, I notice your routine. Early lunch with your husband before he goes to work, right? Then, at 1:00 p.m. up to the roof, right? Back down again, promptly at 1:30, because too much sun is not good for your precious…. Something I need to know right off, dear, no white lies, please. We don't make too much noise up there on the floor above you, do we?…Well, good…Well, good, because I *do* worry. It's just the three of us, the three generations, ha, ha! But we make our share of noise, what with Mother's cane, and Baby Lizbeth crying so much, and my singing on those not very professional tapes to quiet her down…Oh, she's calm now, poor tired thing – her medications have kicked in!…And then, too, the TV, on practically the whole day. It helps to deal with my stress, what with wondering what's to become of us, and man troubles…Man troubles, which I shall *not* burden you with.

SHE *looks back toward her mother.*

I'll only be one short minute more, dear.

Back to her neighbor.

Poor dear…A stroke, yes, a mild one, to be sure, but a stroke, nevertheless…She *has* come a long way, a *long*, long way. Why, she couldn't walk for the longest time…She gets around just fine now, with her special cane…I do have to help her, of course, with–

SHE *lowers her voice to a whisper.*

– personal hygiene and things, if you know what I mean…I don't mind. She's a love.

SHE *turns to her mother again.*

I *don't* mind, do I, love?

SHE *looks at her watch.*

I am not checking my watch out of boredom, Myra, please know that! In 15 minutes, I must handle a very important errand, an errand involving a man named Stewart. Mother will watch Baby Lizbeth for me, won't you, Mother!…Oh, no, Myra, she can and she *will*. She does more than you might think. She *likes* to help because, well, she knows the extra little burden I face with our Baby Lizbeth…No, I'll tell you later, at a more appropriate time…

SHE *laughs.*

Yes, I am! I *am* from the South! How did you *ever* guess? We came up here, my husband, Lester, my *former* husband, Lester, that is, who decided one day he had had enough of corrugated cardboard factories in Georgia, and moved a pregnant wife to corrugated cardboard factories up here, in no man's land, ha, ha!...Well, no, Myra. He took off, just took off, the day he saw our little Lizbeth. I haven't seen him and I *won't* see him, ever again, given the weakly constituted person he showed himself to be!

A beat

Well...there isn't any one name they give it, you see, Myra. The closest they've come up with is "multiple impairments," if you please.

SHE *laughs.*

"Multiple impairments!" Can you bear it? A little precious love with "multiple impairments!" You name it, my poor precious has it: seizures, damaged bodily functioning, poor muscular coordination – *no* muscular coordination is more like it – mental retarda – I don't like to say that word. I prefer "learning difficulties." Yes, you name it, my little Lizbeth has it! And not very pretty to boot! How could that be, I ask sometimes. Not one sign of pity from God? Not one shred of compassion from Him? A trick? A prank to relieve His boredom up there?...Oh, do not misunderstand me. I have *never* thought of Lizbeth as a mistake. No, I think of her as a preparation. He will have her sit at His right side some day!

SHE *laughs.*

"Multiple impairments!" My autobiography! *Twin* burdens, Myra, my two Lizbeths are my twin burdens! I don't mind. I really do *not* mind. They are my two loves as well. A person with two loves is blessed, as I see it. Oh, I *do* thank God for Mother! The minute she heard about our precious, she was here like a shot! She had her health then and was a tower, an absolute *tower* of purpose. "We'll fix that child, Pegeen," she said. "We will make her learn, make her *do*!" And you know, Myra? She meant it! Picture it! At the baby hospital, all those doctors standing around, specialists, as they're called, insisting little Lizbeth would never move, would be a vegetable and never *move*, would die in months. Can you imagine: never *move*, never respond to – what did they call it? "Tactile stimuli?" Meaning she would never respond to *my* touch, her mother's touch! Oh, how wrong they were! My precious knows my touch, welcomes my touch, and knows her Grandma Lizbeth's touch, too, and knows they are different touches! ... Progress, progress was noted. And then, wouldn't you know? Mother got sick herself.

Turning to her mother.

Would you like a cookie, Mother? Of course, you would.

To her neighbor, as SHE *rises.*

Excuse me. I'll be right back.

SHE *heads for her mother's side.* SHE *reaches into the bag and mimes pulling out a cookie and giving it to her mother.*

How about our *younger* Lizbeth? Would she like a cookie, too? Of course, she would.

SHE *kneels at the white blanket.*

Oh, you've got to hold it, my precious. Come on, come on now, reach... No? Not today, little one? Tomorrow, then? Okay! *Tomorrow* you'll learn to reach for it, the way you learned to reach for the red and blue ball with all the shiny stars.

SHE *returns to her neighbor and mimes holding out cookies.*

Shall we forget our diets, Myra?...No? Then, we'll be proud of our remarkable self-denial, won't we?

SHE *sits in her deck chair.*

...Well, yes, Myra. We *are* dressed exactly alike today, the three generations. I made these sundresses. *And* these sunhats. It wasn't difficult – well, not *too* difficult...A picture in a magazine, if you please! I thought to myself, "The sundresses may give a little trouble, but the sun hats will be a breeze!" Proving how wrong I can be! It was the opposite, exactly the opposite!

SHE *laughs.*

If I confess a dream I used to have, Myra, you won't laugh?...When I was younger, I had a nice voice – which today only my little Lizbeth seems to appreciate. And yes, believe it or not, I had a nice shape, too... Oh, thank you, but we both know I could lose ten pounds, fore and aft ...Anyway, since I could also sew, I thought, "Las Vegas is the place for you, Pegeen!" I would be of *double* value, you know? My voice and shape in one of those undemanding chorus lines at night, repairing costumes for the other girls by day!...Well, maybe not sunhats!

SHE *laughs. Then a beat.*

As you can see, I never did get to Las Vegas...What?...Yes, I *have* thought that people looking at us today from the apartment house across the way would not be able to tell the two elder generations apart, would never know which of two identically-dressed femme-fatales on this rooftop had given a cookie, and which was right now eating that cookie?

SHE *laughs.*

Well, they wouldn't see much, anyway. In about ten minutes, as you well know, because you'll go indoors again and I'll go to my errand with the man named Stewart, in ten minutes, that building will cast its long, dark shadow over half this roof, over us and our cookies and our identical sundresses! So much for our glamorous rooftop garden!

SHE *turns to her mother.*

You are watching for crumbs, aren't you, Mother? Poor dear. She is almost asleep. Both my loves like to sleep.

SHE *turns back to her neighbor.*

Glamorous rooftop garden! It could be, if they ever fixed it up, spent money. Why, it can be dangerous, Myra, do you know that? For instance, that spot over there?

SHE *points to the pyramid of bricks.*

I stay away from *that* spot, and you'd do well to stay away from it, too. Don't you see?...You don't? I'll show you.

SHE *goes to the front of the stage and moves the bricks slightly.*

Look. Just *look*! A person who didn't know better? Such a person might go over in a second!

SHE *moves the bricks back to their original place.*

...I *have* spoken to the landlord, Myra, more than once. The man will *not* investigate a couple of loose bricks!...Which reminds me!

SHE *goes back to her mother, but speaks loud enough for her neighbor to hear.*

You have not sneaked anything up here, Mother? Not the red and blue ball with the shiny stars that little Lizbeth loves?...You wouldn't lie to me, Mother? Well, good, then.

SHE *returns to her neighbor.*

...The red and blue ball? Oh, *that*! It was Mother who noticed what Lizbeth liked. She liked strong colors, so Mother went right out and bought this multi-colored ball, complete with shooting stars. And day after day, she rolled that ball around before Lizbeth, and did that precious baby ever get excited! I never saw anyone so – spirited! Before too long, she was reaching for it, sort-of-but-not-quite, creeping toward it, sort-of-but-not-quite. Yes, there was our Lizbeth, straining, pushing, so spiritedly, moving, at long last, at long, long last.

A beat

And there was Mother, even after her mini-stroke, continuing her efforts, working so very hard, *willing* progress for Baby Lizbeth, making a game of it, in spite of her own deficits!

SHE *laughs.*

Reduced to putting that ball into the – oh, what do they call it? – the *crook* of her cane, what a funny word! Pulling it along the floor, encouraging her, no, *demanding* she reach for the red and blue ball with the shooting stars! Oh, yes! Who knows what our Lizbeth can aspire to, if we are patient and loving? That's what Mother has taught me...Yes, she *is* a love. I've only had to speak crossly to her once in our life together. No – twice...What? Well, the first time was – do you really want to hear?...That day, Myra, will I *ever* forget that day? She was watching Lizbeth for me, up here on this very roof, for just a few minutes, when would you believe it? I could *not*! With that cane she was trying to make our Lizbeth reach for her ball – across this roof, you understand!...No, I am *not* kidding...I read the riot act, of course, and she has promised never to do it again.

SHE *turns to her mother.*

You wouldn't lie to me, would you, Mother?

SHE *turns back to her neighbor.*

She is in the land of Nod, poor dear...The *second* time? Well, Myra, it was just last week. I *had* to speak crossly to her again, because of what she did to Stewart, poor man, the man I am going to see in 8 minutes...I met him, you see, a few months ago, and things developed between us, yes, rather quickly. But then – last week, Mother, out of the blue, out of *what* blue I do not know, goes up to Stewart and spits into his face! "Mother!" I said. "What are you doing? This is not Lester. Lester is gone, gone from our lives forever. This is *Stewart*." Mother does get people mixed up sometimes since her mini-stroke, poor dear, but that's no excuse for–

SHE *bursts into tears.*

I'm sorry. I *am* sorry. It's all so difficult!...Stewart, the man I *do* want and *do* need, Myra, is also the man who gave me an ultimatum that day, the ultimatum I am going to answer today, with all the strength I have.

SHE *speaks in her mother's direction.*

Sleep, Mother. Soon, I am going to require your wide-awake attention, to care for Baby Lizbeth, while I answer that cruel ultimatum...

SHE *returns to her neighbor.*

Yes, I'll leave them here together. To show Mother I *do* trust her with my precious. To prove I have forgiven her. To prove my speaking crossly to her was not a permanent indictment.

SHE *tries hard to control her tears now.*

First, Lester, and now Stewart. Can it be, Myra? Can it be that my precious ones are responsible for my losing the only two men I have ever loved? Is it wrong to expect a man to put up with my twin burdens?...Still, my Stewart might have come through for us, might have found a way back to us, except that, you see, suddenly he has been given his chance, his lifetime chance! A cousin, Myra, will sell him a franchise for below cost, far below its worth, says Stewart. And, you just guess where that franchise is! Yes, Las Vegas, of all places! Las Vegas! "You'll come, won't you, Pegeen?" Those were the first words out of his mouth. "Stewart," I said, "of course, we'll come." "No, Pegeen," he said. "I mean you – *alone*." "Alone!" I said. "You've done enough for them," he said. "You still have a nice voice and a nice shape – " those were his exact words! – "you can get into one of those chorus lines. I'll stake you to dancing lessons, or singing lessons, or whatever it takes to get you started." But how could that tempt me? "My twin burdens?" I said. "What of *them*?" "Public institutions," he said. "Public institutions!" I said. "Never. Private places, perhaps, happy private places with sunrooms and gardens." "No," he said. "I will not pay for such places." "Then I cannot and will not think about it." I said. "Suit yourself" he said. "Let me know, because, midweek, at 2:00 p.m., I am gone from here."

A long beat.

I ask you: is that an ultimatum, or isn't it?

Another beat.

Oh, it isn't fair. It is *not* fair. I deserve a life, Myra. Mother is old and sick – she's already *had* a life. And my precious: she will never have a life! Three generations! Only one with the opportunity of happiness and she is not going to have it. Still: there is simply no choice, is there! I know my duty. Yes! In 5 minutes, I will meet that ultimatum of cruelty, and give my decision. Surely you know what that will be, *must* be, Myra!

SHE *brings her hand to her forehead and looks at the sky.*

And, here comes the long, long shadow. Time for you to get your precious Trisha downstairs. Time for me to do what must be done.

SHE *stands.* SHE *heads for the place where the mother sits.*

Look! The dear has dropped her glasses in her sleep.

SHE *slips the glasses into her own pocket.*

Yes, it *has* been nice, Myra. I'll see you again, won't I, on another bright day!

SHE *begins to speak with her mother immediately, so that her departing neighbor will be sure to hear.*

Mother? Mother? It *is* time to wake up, sleepy one. You must be alert, to watch this precious child as you promised, while I do the duty I *must* do.

A beat, while SHE *checks that her neighbor is gone. Now, all at once, stoniness overtakes her face and the cheeriness* SHE *has forced on us, lulling us, vanishes.* SHE *begins the act of murder she has planned.* SHE *whispers to her mother.*

Go ahead and sleep, Mother. It is *important* that you sleep.

SHE mimes kissing her mother's head.

You must never think I don't love you, Mother. I do. But you must do this one thing for me. No one will treat you badly, I promise. They'll think, they'll *know* you didn't mean for it to happen. You were just trying to help again, as always, willing Lizbeth's progress, as always, weren't you! You didn't realize the danger. Of course you didn't! It will just – happen, Mother. Things *do* happen.

A beat

There is no other way. You see?

Certain her mother remains asleep, SHE *takes a cookie from the paper bag and crumbles it in her hand.* SHE *dons the glasses.* SHE *picks up the cane, affecting a limp.* SHE *removes a brightly colored ball from the bag.* SHE *moves to the white blanket.* SHE *picks up the child, and while* SHE *speaks to it, leaves a trail of cookie crumbs behind her.*

Look, precious. See your ball? See it?

SHE puts down the child.

How about music for my precious? You do love your music.

SHE turns on the tape recorder to her soft but scratchy lullaby.

There. Eat your cookie. Isn't it good? Isn't it good?

SHE watches the child eat. After a beat.

If there were another way, my Lizbeth, I would *take* that way, you do know that? Of course, you do. Just as you know I've loved you since the day you were born.

SHE puts the ball into the crook of the cane and, coaxing, drags it along the roof.

Here's your ball. Come and get it, my precious.

SHE moves closer to the edge.

That's it. Reach for your ball now. Come.

SHE *repeats this action, again, then again, executing a kind of crude semi-circle on the roof, each time moving closer to its edge.*

It is only going to take a second, you know. A second, that's all. Afterwards, you'll be in that happy place, where *all* children are smart and they walk and they run, and you'll run with them, my precious, and you'll be the happiest one. *You!* Because you had a mother who sent you there in love. Oh, you are going to sit on His right side, that is my promise. That is what He meant in all this, you see? Without a trace of doubt, I know that that is *exactly* what He meant in all this. What else *could* He have meant?

SHE *is at the edge of the roof now.* SHE *slides the bricks to one side, as we saw her do earlier.*

Come, Lizbeth. Come, my precious. Make your momma proud, proud and happy. You do want your momma to be happy! Of course, you do. Aren't you my precious?

SHE *mimes touching the child's head.*

Want a little more of your cookie? All right. Isn't it good? Isn't it good?

A beat. SHE *watches.* SHE *stands.*

Go on, Lizbeth. Go on.

SHE *stuffs the empty brown paper bag into her pocket.* SHE *"limps" toward her mother.* SHE *drops the glasses into her mother's lap.* SHE *takes one last look at her child.*

It is time now, my precious. It is *time.*

SHE *leaves.*

THE LIGHTS GO DOWN
THE CURTAIN FALLS

www.ingramcontent.com/pod-product-compliance
Lightning Source LLC
Chambersburg PA
CBHW070808100426
42742CB00012B/2289